A CHRISTIAN MANIFESTO
for the
TWENTY-FIRST CENTURY

A CHRISTIAN MANIFESTO
for the
TWENTY-FIRST CENTURY

D. CARLTON O'RORK, DMIN., PHD.

A Christian Manifesto for the Twenty-first Century by D. Carlton O'Rork, Dmin., Phd

This book is written to provide information and motivation to readers. Its purpose is not to render any type of psychological, legal, or professional advice of any kind. The content is the sole opinion and expression of the author, and not necessarily that of the publisher.

Copyright © 2021 by D. Carlton O'Rork, Dmin., Phd

All rights reserved. No part of this book may be reproduced, transmitted, or distributed in any form by any means, including, but not limited to, recording, photocopying, or taking screenshots of parts of the book, without prior written permission from the author or the publisher. Brief quotations for noncommercial purposes, such as book reviews, permitted by Fair Use of the U.S. Copyright Law, are allowed without written permissions, as long as such quotations do not cause damage to the book's commercial value. For permissions, write to the publisher, whose address is stated below.

Printed in the United States of America.

ISBN 978-1-955363-12-9 (Paperback)
ISBN 978-1-955363-13-6 (Digital)

Lettra Press books may be ordered through booksellers or by contacting:

Lettra Press LLC
30 N Gould St. Suite 4753
Sheridan, WY 828011
1 307-200-3414 | info@lettrapress.com
www.lettrapress.com

Contents

Dedication vii
Introduction ix

PART I

Chapter 1   A World Gone Mad 3
Chapter 2   Truth on Trial 13
Chapter 3   History: Pick A Side 23
Chapter 4   Politics: Lions, Tigers, And Bears...Oh My 29
Chapter 5   A Biblical Manifesto Debunking Evolution 38

PART II

Chapter 6   Creeds, Confessions, And Catechisms 51
Chapter 7   God: To Believe Or Not To Believe 61
Chapter 8   The Bible: The Source of All Truth 70
Chapter 9   Jesus Christ: Messiah, Son, Lord 78
Chapter 10 The Spirit of God, The Spirit of Christ,
            The Holy Spirit 88
Chapter 11 "And I Will Build My Church" 98
Chapter 12 Conclusion 111
Chapter 13 Footnotes 123

DEDICATION

This book is dedicated to my now deceased mentors, Francis Schaffer and Dr. Mike Johnston, who have both been the inspiration by way of motivation for this book. And to my spiritual father, Tom Farrell, without whose tireless efforts this would not have come together. And last but not least, Emily and Teresa for the editing and typing and service to the work of the Lord. God bless you all.

To the reader of this book:

Please take your time in reading and consider
the message.

Whether you agree and appreciate the message is beside the point. That you come away understanding it is vital. It will, for some, become immediately obvious by the title alone that the original inspiration for this work was Francis A. Schaeffer's book of similar title A CHRISTIAN MANIFESTO. I decided to tackle this monumental task of following a giant of Christian Apologetics with a fresh look, nearly four decades later, since his work was published by Crossway in 1981.

"Why?", you ask. Well, I wanted to sort of combine a "Manifesto": a written statement declaring publicly the intentions, motives, views, or standards of its issuer, and a "Credo", which comes from the Latin Credo meaning "I believe". And so it follows that a Creed is a statement of beliefs.

We have now crossed the threshold into the twenty first century. Just in the last decade alone we have seen many events play out upon the world stage that would make most folks from forty or fifty years ago gasp in disbelief if they were suddenly thrust forward in time to 2015 - 2020. Over those nearly four decades (since Dr. Schaeffer's book) we have seen the trend of Christendom being split, splintered, shattered, and morphed to such an extreme that it is now nearly unrecognizable from one part of the globe to another. Now its my turn, "Why?"

This book seeks to answer that question and many, many more. I wish to set forth, by way of a manifesto, a creed for all true Christians. I say "true" Christians because not everyone or everything that claims the moniker is indeed true to the name. So buckle up. It may get bumpy in places but hold on tight and I believe in my heart that you will come away from the experience different than you came into it.

INTRODUCTION

The evening news should include a warning disclaimer similar to those about graphic violence;

"WARNING, THIS NEWSCAST MAY CAUSE SEVERE PSYCHOLOGICAL PROBLEMS FOR THOSE OF A WEAKER CONSTITUTION. THE DISCRETION OF A QUALIFIED MENTAL HEALTH PROFESSIONAL IS ADVISED!"

We live in a culture that is in obvious decline; war, pandemic disease, mass killings, religious and political upheaval, terrorism on a global scale. Would even just a couple of generations removed have ever imagined such a world as we now call our everyday? I've heard some say, "it's not that bad. We're just in a 24 hour news cycle these days!" In this modern age Judaeo-Christian values, (upon which this country was founded), are openly mocked and even called hate speech.

Immorality in high places is, not just overlooked, but in many cases is even rewarded in the voting booth. When a Christian takes a stand to halt the rapid decline into chaos we are maligned as intolerant and bigoted. Not every opinion, belief, or way of thinking is right or even true. All views are not valid. Everyone cannot be right. It stands to question then: Who is telling the truth? What is {the} truth?

The Oxford's English Dictionary pronounced the word of the year for 2016 as Post-truth. The definition: "relating to or denoting circumstances in which the objective facts are less influential in shaping public opinion than appeals to emotion and personal belief." So, if I'm understanding the definition, it seems to me that facts just get in the way for some folks. Emotion and personal belief are hoisted high as a standard and rule of the day. Every viewpoint is valid. Every emotion warranted and truth is just a pesky thing that matters little in the public arena. This is what is called Postmodernism (a mutation of liberalism). It's definition is; "A way of thinking where there is no objective, universal truth; there is only the perspective of the group" as follows;

>1~(Liberals, Conservatives, Zionists, Nationalists, etc.) whoever has sway at the time. With the suicide rate at record levels, especially among the young; with mass shootings occurring on a weekly basis; and with natural disasters of epic proportions, it is easy to see why people are on edge about the state our world is in and it's future. One question we see over and over on the news and mumbled through heart wrenching tears is ..."Why, why did this have to happen?" The problems in this 21st century are inescapable. It all comes down to one's worldview. There are poignant questions which shape this personally for every person: "Why are we here?" "What has gone wrong with this world?" (creation/fall) "What can we do to fix the mess?" (redemption). "A worldview is simply the sum total of our beliefs about the world, the 'Big Picture,' that directs our daily decisions and actions."

2~ For example, take the United States, clearly founded on Godly principles and on a book called the Bible; Is she a "Christian Nation as she claims? No! Not by a long shot. There is an old saying that goes, "history is always written by the winner." There is a plethora of versions (viewpoints) of History, Philosophy, Science, Politics, and let's not forget, truth.

When I grew up I practically lived in the library. It was not until my last year of High School that I loosened up to where I would indulge in regular works of fiction. My favorite subjects (in order) were Science and History. Looking back, I was very naive and took "facts" at face value, especially if they came from someone smarter than me. As I entered my late teens that trend began to change. My own estranged mother disowned me when I began to attend a Roman Catholic Church at 14 along with my Step-mom. I took CCD classes for a year and after Baptism & First Communion I became a Roman Catholic. As I began to seriously read my Bible, I noticed some things were not lining up. A resounding question kept nagging at me, "why does the Bible (The word of Almighty God) say one thing and the Pope (Church) say something completely different?" I went to my Parrish's Senior Priest armed with my Bible and some pointed questions. With each question he answered, I countered with just the right scripture to refute it. He threw me out of his office (this was only the first of two times; the other being six years later in the U. S. Navy). This was a major blow to me, and this on top of my mother's silence towards me.

Around age fifteen I realized I was smarter than the average bear. I set out on a quest for truth. I resolved that God, the creator said He does NOT lie. As I remember, my mother did always seem to trust that premise. Science, as taught by men, had let me down. Even as the School textbooks tried to proffer Evolution as fact, I knew it was a sham full of holes! With so many versions of History, Religion, Science, etc., out there, who do you trust? The quest I mentioned earlier actually began at eight years old in a small country church. Even so young, I knew something was missing and this preacher, on this fine Spring morning, said he had the answer . . . Jesus! I walked that long aisle to investigate; to go get this Jesus in my heart! This was the answer, but it did not come to fruition until thirty nine years later. It (faith) finally clicked for me. This Jesus is the one who claimed HE was, "the way, the truth, and the life . . ."(John 14:6). I had always been taught that Science had all the answers, right? This planet, positioned just at the perfect distance from our Sun which itself is the perfect size and temperature and age, all to support life, a vast and very precise universe. . .Wow! You mean to tell me all of this just went BANG, and came into being? And what about the amazingly complex lifeforms with man at the pinnacle, clearly separate and apart from any other "animal" ? You mean to tell me this all happened by chance? did I hear someone say Evolution was fact; what? How is a theory a fact?

So, who is right? Who has the truth? Pontius Pilate, the man who sent Jesus Christ to the cross, asked a similar question, "What is truth?" (John 18:38) He was standing right there with the essence of truth - Truth personified. Jesus once said in an awesome prayer to the Father, "Your word is truth." (John 17:17).

One can try (and many have) to dismantle this truth that is the Word of God, the Bible. That the Bible is historically accurate is, in this day and age, incontrovertible. This does not necessarily mean it is inspired, but if it isn't then it is the work of a genius beyond any we've ever seen. We know the Bible itself claims to be the word of God. The once Christian hater turned Apostle, Paul once said scripture is "God breathed" (Greek - Theopneustos).

Many, when faced with the veracity and proclaimed authority of the word of God, use the Serpent's method to circumvent responsibility to sacred precepts: create doubt and cast it out. To put confidence in man is certainly folly; as is evident by all the so-called "answers" out there! One can take a walk down through the ages and ask, "do we trust": Buddha, Aristotle, Plato, Muhammad, Nietzsche, Kant, Marx, and the list could go on and on. Or do we trust the one who is the reason for everything (Romans 3:4 God)? I'd rather err on the side of God. That same Paul even told the folks at Rome, "let God be true, but every man a liar." (Romans 3:4 KJV). Man has always had a fascination with "so-called" wisdom. The word Philosophy means love of wisdom, but man is ultimately quite fallible and very selfish. Most of us are well aware of the beast within, even if we esteem ourselves good, we know the truth. Many though, don't seem to know of common grace which is the means by which God, through His infinite wisdom and His mighty power, sustains creation, holding back sin and evil, as it would tend to overwhelm all of creation like a flood.

Those who followed Christ were called "Christians" in derision, but we use it today as a positive moniker for true believers. As true believers and children of God we still have that fallen nature. Sometimes it manifests when we least expect it. We have a responsibility not to lose faith in the Lord or ourselves. It is up to us to show the world that Christianity is not merely a religion or simply some system of belief designed for only certain people. It is a story of redemption which began in a beautiful Garden and continues beyond this planet into forever spent in a brilliant city provided by the one who created us to enjoy it right there with Him.

Only Christianity offers a comprehensive worldview that can successfully answer every aspect of human life and creation. Only a relationship with the one who created us for such, offers a way to live free of condemnation, fear, and self loathing in such a cynical world. If Christians are to carry the life giving message of redemption in Christ, they must first understand their faith and then live it out in daily life. The Bible is full of the people of God who have failed and failed big. It is all right there for us to see and learn from. In the Christian faith itself there has developed a confusing array of messages, methods, programs, movements, and denominations that I believe Jesus himself would not condone. The early Christians saw a critical need to have agreement on certain basic tenets for the universal (invisible) Church. In the late 4th century A.D.; councils were convened to develop a single unifying Creed. Thus were born the Nicean Creed and from it the shorter one many know as the Apostles Creed. The need was critical because of rampant false teaching and heresy very common then, just as it is today. The creed gave the Councils a way to provide a solid foundation upon which core Christian doctrine could rest, yet in simple form.

A Creed is all well and good. It has a place and value, but in this tumultuous world we need something more; if not another Reformation, then a strong and clear statement - a manifesto. A clarion call to cut through all the voices, books, programs, schools of Theology. To cut to the chase of what it is to be a Christian in heart, soul, mind, and being. We need something to let the world know that there is a standard. There is also a way to live up to it, but this way is not grasped by human hands, but by supernatural means - by a work of God in the heart of man to bring him back to the intended state of relationship with his awesome creator Father. Continue on and learn what a Manifesto for the 21st century looks like.

Dr. D. Carlton O'Rork, D Min.

All Biblical references in this book are taken from the King James Bible.

PART I

Chapter 1

A WORLD GONE MAD

"Most fundamentally, our culture, society, government and law are in the condition they are in, not because of a conspiracy, but because the church has forsaken its duty to be the salt of the culture. It is the church's duty (as well as its privilege) to do now what it should have been doing all the time – use the freedom we do have to be the salt of the culture." From A Christian Manifesto by Francis A Schaeffer

We're living in uncertain times. This simple fact can't be argued. Just in the last decade (2010 - 2020) we've seen some scary events cause great alarm across the globe. Ebola Virus went from epidemic to pandemic when it came to the U.S.; The Zika Virus scare; Gas prices skyrocketed topping $4 a gallon; Giants of the financial, banking, and automotive sectors got bailed out when faced with folding and by, of all entities, the U.S. Government! Oh, there's more…Swine Flu was declared, "a public health emergency." A Healthcare reform nightmare called "Obamacare" was enacted; "Don't' ask, Don't tell" repealed.[1]

Most of us are well aware of the numerous natural disaster events: Earthquakes, Tsunamis, Monster Hurricanes (and typhoons) many of which shattered some long held records. We are all also painfully aware of Terror groups like Al-Shabab, Boko Haram, and ISIS. There are some indelible stories which stain the fabric of our memories to the point where we wonder, " why have things gotten so bad?" The stories I have shared and am about to further share are but a small sampling, giving rise to my title choice for this chapter.

Dateline: December 12, 2018 NBC Nightly News with Lester Holt: The topic was the Opioid epidemic in the U.S. As of the close of 2016 there were 18,000 opioid overdose deaths. This is up 139% since only 2013! As of early December 2018 Fentanyl outstretched heroine as the most dangerous drug in the U.S.

The very next night on the same news broadcast: By year end 2017 there had been 39,775 gun deaths this up from only 10,000 in 1990! There is not enough time or space in this work to list the numerous jaw dropping stories and events of just the last few decades. The most significant in my recent memory is 9/11/2001. In the early morning hours two hijacked commercial airliners struck the World Trade Center Twin Towers in New York City in the {absolute} worst ever terrorist attack on American soil. A third hijacked airliner destroyed a huge part of the Pentagon and a fourth was forced to crash in a field near Shanksville, PA. Some 3000 people were killed, including those (2750) at the Twin Towers.

Terrorism has now become an everyday occurrence prompting one National News network to create a "Terrorism Alert Desk" segment so as to run down a laundry list of new and emerging terror threats, plots, and events. Oh, but there's more:

June 2009 a sitting President proclaimed the month of June as LGBT (lesbian, gay, bisexual, and transgender) month. During the proclamation he called on America to support homosexual rights! This same President [Barak Obama] once said, "whatever we once were, we are no longer just a Christian nation; we are also a Jewish nation, a Muslim nation, a Buddhist nation, a Hindu nation ... a nation of nonbelievers." [2] In 2015 The United States Supreme Court in a landmark decision ruled in Obegefell vs Hodges that state bans on same-sex marriage violated same-sex couples rights under the due process and equal protection clauses of the fourteenth amendment. [3] On March 23 2016 Gov. Pat McCrory (R) of North Carolina signed the "bathroom bill" providing that people use state facilities corresponding to their birth certificate gender. Implementation was suspended by a Federal Judge in response to numerous boycotts and the U.S. Departments of Justice and Education, on May 13, issuing guidance advising public schools to allow students to use the facilities matching their gender identity! [4]

On another note: By year's end 2016 there were 45,000 suicides in this Country; which is an increase of 30% compared to 20 years ago! This made suicide the second leading cause of death and that number was more than double the homicides.[5] Has the world gone mad? To me this seems an appropriate question. As I mentioned in the introduction, if one from the Forties or Fifties were to be brought forward in time to this year (2020), they would think Armageddon to be right at the door-step and worldwide nuclear war a "when" and not an "if". If the time travelers were from the U.S. they would be almost certain that America had long lost her moral compass.

This is no longer a country where "In God We Trust" is even remotely true! have we forgotten our roots? Pardon me as I focus on America for a bit. You know, The United States of America who threw caution to the wind, took a stand risking life, limb, and possessions to throw off the tyrant Great Britain. Religious liberty brought most all of the newcomers in the very early years of colonization. It was the reason they came and faith was their foundation. First we saw Roanoke, then the first successful group at Jamestown, whose charter from King James included, "the propagating of the Christian religion" in the new world. Then, 16 years later, just before the Pilgrims even made their landing, they drew up the Mayflower Compact which was a document designed as a covenant to state purpose and guidance for civil law which they understood to be based on faith in God as evidenced by the following, "Having undertaken, for the glory of God, and advancement of the Christian Faith, and honor of our

King and Country, a voyage to plant the first colony in the Northern parts of Virginia..." The Pilgrims purposed to be self governed under God first and foremost. That was 150 years before the Declaration of Independence!

It is a fact that the United States, like it or not, had predominantly Christian roots from its beginnings and during its founding. The foundational laws and all founding documents are irrefutably based on the Holy Bible! I get the feeling that there are some who are, as yet, unconvinced. Allow me to offer the following examples from History beside the two we've already seen: The Massachusetts Charter penned in 1629 had this line, "...obedience of the only true God and Savior of mankind and the Christian faith..." And while we are here in Massachusetts, let me mention a very stark fact: that Puritan New England not only based their law and government on Holy Scriptures, but they produced the very first widely accepted textbook for school-age children called the New England Primer whose alphabet lessons were developed solely on the Holy Bible [6]. Imagine that! The Bible taught in schools!, what was the Country coming to?

But wait, there's more: 1638-39 The Fundamental Orders of Connecticut reads, "...there should be an orderly and decent government established according to God...to maintain and preserve the liberty and purity of the gospel of our Lord Jesus Christ which we now profess...which is practiced amongst us." There are many more, but let me shift focus now to schools of higher learning which were established on the very same principles of the Christian Faith. Harvard (1638) was founded by Massachusetts Puritans. Clearly outlined in the "Rules and Precepts" of 1646 as one of the enrollment requirements we find, "Every one shall consider the main end of his life and studies to know God and Jesus Christ which is eternal life...". Yale, Princeton and Dartmouth (all established 1701-1754) were all founded to train pastors and missionaries to propagate the gospel of Jesus Christ! To see any of these schools today, you would not ever have guessed them to have been founded on the Word of God.

I would like to quote a great Bible Teacher, Dr. Mike Johnston for whom this work is partially dedicated: "America was founded upon Biblical principles including the sanctity of life (Ex. 21:22- 24; Psalm 139) [all versions as paraphrased] and traditional marriage represented by one man and one woman for one lifetime (Gen. 2:22- 24), [all versions as paraphrased]. Now both of these have been deftly destroyed (Obegefell vs Hodges) by God hating liberals who choose filth over faith, and rights over righteousness. As a result, America, once vibrantly Christian, has now become, "the universal habitation of devils."[7]

The above statement highlights two of the most heinous sins in the book (Bible) - Murder, especially of the innocent or helpless and Homosexuality: "Thou shalt not lie with mankind as with womankind: it is an ABOMINATION... defile not ye yourselves in any of these things..." (Lev. 18:22). Many spurn the Bible pointing out that God is a vicious God because he commanded the Israelites to utterly destroy the inhabitants of Canaan their "Promised Land". Some may think this unjustified, but many completely overlook the reasons God gave. He told them (Israelites) many, many times to avoid the abominations of the heathen which included human sacrifice (Murder) and gross unabashed and unnatural sexual acts. The King James translators chose the word "heathen" and not "Gentiles" because of the Biblical context and their view of the Hebrew word 'goyim' to describe these people who exercised no control over any of their appetites and passions.

Herein is the rub. Abram who God renamed Abraham was promised, through his posterity, the land of Canaan, but that also his posterity would need to reside in another land, "know for a surety that thy seed shall be a stranger in a land that is not theirs..." 430 years so that the abominations of the Canaanites (heathen) could reach its full fervor and God's people could be protected from such an evil influence. An influence that allowed sexual perversion by mandate of law and murder was excused as ritual making it quite legal. Sound a bit familiar? Abortion, like it or not, is murder! DNA proves that life begins at conception. It really has nothing to do with "rights." If it did, along with me many would ask, "what about the child's rights?" The heathen in the land of Canaan did not believe in the one true God of the Hebrews nor did they accept his word. As in the days of Noah. They did, "only evil continually" (Gen. 6:5). Again I say, sound familiar?

One of my favorite Christians is Ken Ham who is CEO and President of Answers in Genesis. In 2009 he gave an address called "Understanding The Times: An Urgent Call to Return to Our Biblical Foundations." The following is an excerpt from that address;

> "In recent history, America has been the greatest Christian nation on earth. It has the largest number of seminaries, churches, Christian colleges, Christian radio and TV stations and other Christian resources. Just visit any Christian publishing convention and you will see an astounding number of resources. More than ever in the history of our country. But for all of that, America is becoming less Christian every day. The church is supposed to affect the culture, but it seems, and quite unfortunately so, the culture is invading the church."

Allow me to digress back to our discussion on our founding for just a moment. July 4th 1776 the early draft of the Declaration of Independence had but two signers; John Hancock, who was President of Congress and Charles Thompson, Secretary of Congress. On July 8th, four days later, members of congress took the document out on to the steps of Independence Hall and read it aloud in proclamation to the City of Philadelphia. At conclusion of the reading, the Liberty Bell was rung. The bell had an inscription around the top of it; A quote from Leviticus 25:10 (KJV), "Proclaim liberty throughout all the land unto all the inhabitants thereof." - What, isn't that from the Bible? At an official government function?

Yes,...Yes indeed! The very fabric of our nation is most certainly intricately woven from seam to seam with unmistakable professions, proclamations, prayers and confessions of faith in God, the Bible and in Jesus Christ.

The following is an excerpt from some of the mountain of material at Wallbuilders;

> "The sixteen Congressional proclamations for prayers and fasting throughout the American Revolution were not vague, obtuse or bland (i.e., the acknowledgment of Jesus Christ, quoting from Romans 14;17); however, this is not at all unusual considering the prominent role that many ministers played in the Revolution and our very founding as a free and independent nation."

One memorable example is John Peter Muhlenburg (note his first and middle names), who once delivered a passionate sermon on Ecclesiastes 3 to his congregation. When he got to verse 8 he emphasized where it says, "a time of war and a time of peace," he curtly noted that this was not a time of peace, it was a time of war. Then as his entire congregation fixed their gaze upon him, he threw off his clerical robes, underneath he was wearing the uniform of a commissioned officer in the Continental Army! He marched to the back of the church, ordered a particular drumbeat and 300 recruits joined him that very day.

As each July 4th rolls around, it seems that Americans are more concerned with the next party or the best fireworks than with the actual celebration of the forefather's hard fought victory which birthed this nation. I was, for many years, guilty of the same distractions. Now that I know Jesus, I can't be so shallow. Now that I see the very foundations of a great and powerful nation eroding and crumbling before my very eyes, I have to sound an alarm! This is by no means a "Chicken Little" mentality as some may assert! This is quite serious and I am sure I am not alone.

Preserving American liberty depends first upon our understanding the foundations on which our (still) great nation was built and then preserving (not tossing out or blotting out or crying "separation of church and state") the principles on which it was founded. Let's not let the purpose for which we were established be forgotten. As Wallbuilder's said, "The founding fathers have passed us a torch; let's not let it go out..." also as pointed out... "If the foundations be destroyed, what can the righteous do?" (Psalm 11:3)

Speaking of Separation of Church and State, did you know that, much like unicorns, there is no such thing. I'll come back to this in a bit; first I want to paint a picture of this country from a different angle. In case it hasn't already become obvious, I am an unapologetic conservative and fundamentalist. Society these days has a flawed idea of what a fundamentalist is so I'll give a brief definition here. A fundamentalist from a purely Christian perspective is - a Bible believing, Christ exalting man/woman of God who believes and sticks to the fundamentals of our faith while also opposing Modernism (liberalism) and Worldliness. I offer this because I am about to go in a direction that will touch on politics, liberals, conservatives, democrats, and republicans.

There is a left and a right, a far left and an extreme right wing. On the liberal side (they like to be called progressives) we find the ACLU, Planned Parenthood, Democrats and other godless politicians, homosexuals, feminists, and the LGBTQ crowd, all of which have long been waging an all out war on Christianity. Most of these folks believe they can be their own God. They have hated anything that even looks Christian and have marked anyone who disagrees with them as bigots and extremists. For decades their efforts had been somewhat subversive and stealthy, but there is solid evidence in recent years of an intentional effort to thwart, hush, and otherwise silence Christians and remove them and their influence from the public sector at any cost. Of late Christian business people with faith and values are being vilified, boycotted and hauled into court because they oppose what society at large has always known, for centuries, was clearly unnatural and just plain wrong!

The assault is on. The battle cry of the liberal (extreme) left to stifle and stop the Christian right "by law", as they say, is now being realized in the old saying, "Separation of Church and State". As I stated earlier, there is no such thing. These secular government-as-savior humanists say they want their children protected from obsolete Christian ideals and to have freedom from religion - not freedom of religion.

Vic Bilson of Jeremiah Project said this: "liberal activists would have us believe our Founding Fathers were terrified at the prospect of Christians participating in the political process. This led them, we're told, to establish a wall of separation between church and state. But, no such provision appears in the Constitution or any of the founding documents. The principle is found only in one of Thomas Jefferson's letters, and referred, not to the exclusion of religious people from government, but to the protection of religion from governmental interference."

To quote Dr. Mike Johnston once again on this subject: "...'Religious' in the founding era meant something other than it does today (Liberals loathe this, because it removes the choke- hold they try to keep on religious freedoms). The Founding Fathers understood "religious" as pertaining to a particular denomination." This is one reason why the Bill of Rights was added to our Constitution -- to limit the power of government. The easiest way to understand the First Amendment is that it restricted Congress from establishing "The First Baptist Church of America" and then forcing membership.

My dear reader please remember that, although America has changed, -- God hasn't! His Word hasn't, and won't ever change. By themselves, the founding documents provide undeniable evidence of our obvious Christian origins. The question is not, "has America (and the world) gone downhill morally?" But it is, "just how far is our decline?" My question: how did we get here? Keep reading and you will see some crystal clear indicators as to how.

Chapter One individual study/group discussion questions;

What is happening in the world now that gives you pause to consider how close we are to the last of the last days?

How do you respond in conversations about controversial laws such as LGBTQ legislation and anti-conversion therapy? Do you even contribute?

Does it surprise you to learn that, "Separation of Church & State," is not really a part of our Founding documents?

Chapter 2

TRUTH ON TRIAL

"Justice is turned back, and righteousness stands afar off; for truth is fallen in the streets, and equity can not enter. So truth fails, and he who departs from evil makes himself a prey." (Isaiah 59:14-15)

The Bible prophet Isaiah said the above 2700 years ago. His indictment (Inspired by God) was against a society that had been founded upon God, faith, and the Word of the LORD. That society, though part of the ancient world, had the same problems with truth that we have in our day. Yes, times have changed there can be no doubt. The changes since Isaiah's day are quite dramatic in comparison, but people have not changed. Our toys and our weapons have, but we haven't; neither has God who is the absolute source of all truth. So guess what? Truth has not changed either, that is until . . . changed by man!

Someone once said to me, " you have your truth, and I have mine." This person was well under 40 and was an obvious product of our American public school system which has, for decades, indoctrinated our youth with a strong sense of RELATIVISM. Relativism basically says a claim is true relative to the beliefs or values of an individual or group that accepts it. To put it another way: Relativism is a state or condition where there is no transcendent source of {moral} truth. ..(no standard) and people are left to construct truth (morality) on their own. For many there really is no distinction, but, for those on the opposing side, there most certainly is. These hold that truth does not vary from person to person, group to group; they accept absolute truth also known as objective truth. Those who hold this view believe people discover truth and do not create it. Reality quantifies a claim by evidence regardless if it is accepted by anyone.

Truth has been quite the victim in the vast panorama of human drama. For those fond of the sciences, engineering and logic, truth is like mathematics, pure, set, and unalterable. It has a base, a standard. This is the complete opposite of relativism. One of my favorite authors, John MacArthur, who authored the award winning notes in the MacArthur Study Bible, wrote a fantastic and thought provoking book "The Truth War" in 2007 (Thomas Nelson). On the back cover is this, "Right now, truth is under attack, and much is at stake. Perhaps no one in America is more passionate than John MacArthur about exposing those who are mounting this attack - especially those bringing the assault right into the church." Well, guess what? That publisher hasn't met me. Anyone who knows me well can tell you that I have a fierce passion for Truth and for God's Word.

This quest I have been on since my mid teens (over 40 years now), has taught me one valuable lesson. People lie! There was a TV show called House. The main character, Dr. Gregory House, was a brilliant diagnostician. In one episode with a particularly chaotic brain storming session with his interns he said, "when you keep getting jerked around by what is presenting before your eyes and what the patient tells you, then there is only one thing to remember . . . everyone lies!" I never forgot that episode. This keen observation, although from a fictional character, holds true in all areas of life. Try an experiment (I've done this) to see if this is true or not. Think back to all of the people in your life whom you have known well and who have known you well. Are they people you could point to, and with absolute certainty, you could say that this person never lied.

Parents, spouses, siblings, best friends, and everyone I could think of. I also applied the thought, "would they fudge on their taxes -- would they tell their spouse that the clothes they are happily modeling are hideous when asked, 'how do I look?'" -- and on and on. I came to the conclusion -- everyone does lie!

It really is simple to understand. Fallen man lies because selfishness runs at our core; especially those without a standard, without objective truth found only in our creator; those without God! We know deep inside that God and Truth are one and the same - (remember "it is impossible for God to lie" Heb. 6:18).

In the book "Atheist Manifesto" by Michel Onfray, I saw an arrogant and abject disdain for God by this man. So it was not at all surprising to find him rejecting God's truth as well. Onfray paints his malcontent for God and religion with a broad brush even in the face of undeniable facts from Bible History whose veracity has long been well established. This tendency is true of most secularists and socialists. This consummate atheist, it was obvious, hated the very idea of objective truth and reading his work gave me a very familiar lead weight in the pit of my stomach. I get that same feeling when I read books from science and evolutionary theory, from the various philosophies, and from the godless liberals in the media and government (you know, the ones who advocate for the murder of the innocent unborn and who embrace the abomination of homosexuality). The foregoing has the answer as to why truth is on trial. It answers, at least partly, why our world has so many "versions" of truth.

The selfishness of mankind is an ugly thing and can be seen all around. Just take a drive on any major interstate highway and in no time at all you can witness in raw fashion the audacity of man to get his way or be so wrapped up in his own life that he doesn't even notice how many people he has cut off, tailgated, or otherwise angered as he goes carelessly about his own business. We will look at philosophy, history, politics, and science to see some of the "versions" of so called truth from each. My own journey, I've mentioned, has brought me to where the real treasure is. As I said, even as a confused teen, I knew God to be right and man, pretty much wrong. This gave me my base, my standard -- The Holy Bible! MacArthur said, " a biblical perspective of truth also necessarily entails the recognition that ultimate truth is an objective reality. Truth exists outside of us and remains the same regardless of how we may perceive it. Truth by definition is as fixed and constant as God is immutable."[1] Francis Schaeffer, the inspiration for this book, called truth like this "true truth" and said it was the unchanged and unchanging expression of who God is -- it is never our own interpretation of reality."

Okay, I can't keep going on this topic without some clarity --

some sort of definition. The Merriam-Webster's entry for truth is: "the real state of things, the body of real events - actuality, a true or accepted statement or proposition, and finally, agreement with fact of reality - correctness." The American Heritage Dictionary at its 4th entry says, "4. Theo. & Philo. - That which is considered to be the ultimate ground of reality."[2] This last entry struck me in that it actually had a theological and philosophical perspective.

Philosophy in its basic sense is, "the study of the nature, causes, or principles of reality, knowledge, or values, based on logical reasoning."[3] When we shave this down to a finer point we see philosophy as the sum of the ideas and convictions of an individual or group (e.g. His philosophy of kindness...).

Philosophy is not merely the domain of the eccentric and brilliant who reside in caves or on some remote mountaintop as many have believed it to be. It is what we as humans do when not frantically striding out the hamster wheel of daily life. Remember the last time you gazed up with wonder on a cloudless night at the starry expanse? The thoughts which we entertain about matter, energy, light, and existence can make for some deep reflection.

Then our gaze comes back home to our world as we meditate and cogitate our place in it all. That, my friend, is philosophy in action. So we are all philosophers at some point or other in our lives.

> Philosophy is not so much about coming up with answers to fundamental questions as it is about the process of trying to find these answers. To put a finer point on it, for this amateur philosopher, as it is for many philosophers who have gone before, it is about the process which becomes necessary in the face of so many ideas and versions of the truth. Truth has been on trial since mankind showed up on this planet. Everyone can't be right. Some surely seem more right than others, but who is to say?

While in the study of Philosophy, I ran across a humorous story about the subject: "There were these two men drinking beer together. One of them held his glass of beer up to the light, scrutinized it thoughtfully, then observed, 'Life is like a glass of beer.' His companion looked up at the glass, turned to his friend, and asked, 'Why is life like a glass of beer?' 'How should I know?' the other answered, 'I'm not a philosopher.'"[4] Philosophers over the centuries have devoted themselves to the contemplation of the problems of this world; some in a scientific approach like Rene Descartes, and some in a broadly abstract way like Aristotle.

Many could not have known the impact they would have on whole societies. Such men as Marx, Thomas Jefferson, John Stuart Mill could not have imagined their ideas forming enduring materials which became foundations for such ideologies as Communism on the one hand, and Democratic societies on the other.

Philosophers have, as a whole, shared a common thread of conviction that a deep look within and careful analysis of our core views, along with our evidence for them, are worthwhile and have great value. Those who have engaged in such introspection and have become famous for recording their results, think in certain ways. We have the benefit of their legacy as we peruse where their meditations have led them. These great men have been curious, as I have, as to what we base our knowledge on, then what standards are employed in arriving at sound judgments?

Which beliefs should we cling to and cherish and which should be cast aside? The serious philosopher (or seeker of truth) has a strong compulsion to find the right answers, those that any rational person can feel are warranted after due diligence and careful consideration. The fact that some answers have been offered, those accepted by the majority in a given society, does not satisfy the philosopher. Even though those or certain other answers may "feel" like the right ones is not enough as a basis for relying upon them. Philosophers try to arrive at certainty of rightness before an expectation that a rational person can adopt the concepts as their own.

Philosophy on a personal level makes a person think and reflect on the very foundations of their outlook, their knowledge, and their beliefs. This journey of self discovery and introspection most all of us take at one time or another, makes us question the reasons for what we accept or don't as well as the importance of our ideals in the hope that our final convictions, which can be arrived at in our lifetime in a very fluid way, will be rationally held ones. As I mentioned earlier, it is a popular misconception that the philosopher is a solitary and reclusive thinker arriving at conclusions in isolation, but this is actually rarely the case.

Philosophy is an intricate mosaic of topics such as politics, morality, religion, etc., and has been examined, debated, analyzed, codified, such that multitudes of volumes adorn library shelves.

Literally thousands of schools of philosophy have been erected, societies shaped, and revolutions sparked all from what at times may appear self evident and other times paradoxical and devoid of common sense. The philosophers themselves which have left their mark on history are quite distinct in personalities. Some were optimistic like Confucius, some despairing and cynical like Buddha. Some were meticulous and painstaking like Socrates and Aristotle and others thought and wrote in broad strokes like Kierkegaard and Marx. The ideas and systems of thought of these great men who have gone before us are as varied as those stars up in the night sky I mentioned earlier.

The various ideologies and schools of thought are: Ancient philosophy, revolutionary, contemporary, stoicism, nihilism, existentialism, rationalism, humanism, modernism, and finally, postmodernism. This list is by no means exhaustive. This shows us just how complex life and existence is as is the search for truth within that framework. It can certainly feel like grasping at straws. Why are there so many views, systems, beliefs, and schools of thought? Whenever one tries to answer these questions in an academic way, it becomes obvious that, as a wise old man used to always say, "there's too many cooks in the kitchen."   Philosophy in and of itself is not a bad thing. Where it has led some in their thinking has proven disastrous. The search for ultimate truth is a worthy goal, but at some point we must stand in awe of Creation as it offers proof (only for those Willing to accept it) of a powerful someone with massive intelligence behind all that we can see in the natural world. Paul said to the Romans, "For since the creation of the world His invisible attributes (His divine nature) have been clearly seen, being understood by the things that are made, even His eternal power and Godhead, so that they are without excuse." (Romans 1:20)

Far too many have tried to set their own standard and topple the foundations which have existed for thousands of years that make for strength and stability in a given society. Truth is indeed under attack. The opening scripture bears repeating at this point.

"And judgment is turned away backward, and justice standeth afar off: for truth is fallen in the street and equity cannot enter.

Yea truth faileth; and he that departeth from evil maketh himself a prey, and the LORD saw it, and it displeased Him that there was no judgment." (Isaiah 59:14-15) Here we have a society who consistently ignored God's truth and accepted a substitute. Their alternative was to accept the lies and false hopes of the dominant culture of the pagans surrounding them. Isaiah was so exasperated with these stubborn and selfish people that, under Holy Spirit inspiration he said,

"...judgment is turned away backward..." This means that there were no longer boundaries. God gave his precepts and laws to set well established boundaries for successful living within the communities of the Nation of Israel! Those proper and pure boundaries had eroded so much that justice was forced to "...stand afar off..." There was no place for pure justice and righteousness in a land filled with selfishness, sin, and lies (what is not truth is a lie). Truth can't even occupy its rightful place in public places. So far had they turned their backs that even traditional places of worship had become pagan alters and dens of sexual deviance and debauchery! Truth had indeed "...fallen in the street..." Does any of this sound a bit familiar?

America and the World have gone the same way. That which was unthinkable only a generation ago is now commonplace and if one decides to swim against the tide of evil he, "... makes himself a prey...", a victim. Truth, in our modern day is all but in a coffin. She is absent from her rightful place in our public places like government, Schools, and especially the media! Evil runs rampant in all sectors from Main Street to Wall Street. Woe to you if you decide to follow your conscience - your faith! We've seen a baker vilified in the media and forced to close the doors while spending thousands in a needless legal battle over something that was once not even up for debate. One woman was even jailed for taking a stand on same sex marriage!

Much like society at large in Isaiah's day 2700 years ago, people have chosen their own path, their own truth abandoning their well established foundations. The passage from Isaiah applies today just as much, if not more, than it did oh so many years ago. Today the trend is called Postmodernism. In general, this is the tendency to dismiss the possibility of any sure and settled knowledge of the truth or truth in general. In "The Truth War" John MacArthur said this about Postmodernism: "Postmodernism suggests that if objective truth exists, it cannot be known objectively or with any degree of certainty. That is because (according to Postmodernists) the subjectivity of the human mind makes knowledge of objective truth impossible."

In today's public arena strong convictions about any point of truth are judged extremely arrogant and grossly naive. The very notion of evil, for example, does not easily fit into the Postmodern mindset of secular society. In an age of "tolerance" and "diversity" - one of acceptance of everyone - competing claims of truth are not only not tolerated their destruction is sought. There is today a relentless drive, which was once rather stealthy, to suppress, redact, and remove any dogma, doctrine, creed or law which does not serve the Postmodern schematic for a secular society - a godless society.

Next, let's see what effects History has suffered at the hands of this same society.

Chapter two individual study/group discussion questions

Do you think people are mostly truthful? Why?

Why does the world hate the truth of God, His Word and His Son?

Has the Creation ever caused you to consider its origin? What were you taught about it?

Chapter 3

HISTORY: PICK A SIDE

"Great thanks, laud, and honor ought to be given unto the clerks, poets, and historiographers that have written many noble books of wisdom of the lives, passions, and miracles of holy saints, of histories of noble and famous acts, and of chronicles since the beginning into this present time, by which we be daily informed and have knowledge of many things of whom we should not have known if they had not left to us their monuments written." Wm Claxton (1484)

I want to talk about history as it is a subject that seems to have a myriad of facets and deeply entrenched perspectives depending on who you ask (or read). There is no way this one chapter can hope to do justice to the complexity and scope. My purpose then is to show how sometimes things are not always as they have been written. In this age of "slide-rule" truth there is brought to bear a sense of incredulity as to whether the central concerns of history as truth-telling is free of agenda driven bias. Herodotus first used the term historia (inquiry) for our modern word history and from his epics, its obvious that Homer was one to assess and judge based on facts as a result of diligent examination. So its relatively easy to see that there is a definite connection between study and history going way back into ancient times.

History is a broad subject, but it can manifest in very specific niche works like, "A History of Germanic Peoples", A Brief History of the World", or "The Real History of the American Revolution", to name just a few. But, is the study of history, as one pursues its facts and stories, a science or an art? To R.G. Collingwood who wrote the classic, "The Idea of History," rules or structure are anathema. As I delved into the world of history by pulling and reading numerous tomes of every range and type, I found that the history of historiography as viewed from the perspective of a zeal for the truth reveals a spectrum and not any one hard and fast set of rules. Some of the great historians who saw history as an absolute search for truth based on an a set of available facts were, like me, sticklers for truth and of the camp that calls pure historical pursuit a science. But, even we sticklers must admit there are also valuable works from the other side (the artists) too. No matter which side you choose one will find agendas. It can't be avoided.

Philosophy, Sociology, Politics, Nationalism and the like affect all the great pursuits like history, science, politics, etc. History isn't immune to such influences. History, among the others, has shown itself to be Republican, Christian, Jewish, Socialist, Marxist, Liberal, and on and on. Here too we see a very colorful spectrum with no one dominating, but, again, many versions to choose from depending on how deep you go. Still, being agenda driven, is what we've been told the truth?

Many of our modern historians have come from the halls of our great University system which tends in many cases to manipulate the student of history making him a scientist on the search for facts and details no matter the conclusions. A purely clinical approach can have its own drawbacks. As with any area of scholarly pursuit, one must approach the facts first, but also feel free to be inquisitive as to the why and how of human behavior. This is something that is not always gleaned from broken pottery shards or stone foundation remnants, but from the great epics and fanciful tales of a particular culture.

At best the archaeologist and the scientists can only speculate until the uncovered evidence is weighed in the balance of the narratives preserved by countless generations. When it comes to the biased accounts and agenda laden tales we can't just throw the baby out with the bathwater. We should be like the philosopher and keep a measure of healthy skepticism.

One historian gave me pause when he gave a perfect example of speculation gone awry. There was a time when there were some sites in Ireland which yielded some very intriguing articles of obvious Roman origin. As two respected archaeologists speculated on the possibilities, they settled on a Roman invasion of Celtic lands. This did not match up with either the historical record nor the dated time period. They were stumped, as was the scientific community. Then a Celtic historian spoke up and solved the mystery. She pointed out in a piece she had published in a well respected historical journal, that the discovery actually made good sense when you consider this particular people weren't farmers, or metal workers, nor other known professions for this culture, but they were more than likely merchants who traveled to nearby ports to trade with seafarers and other merchants who wanted wool and other wares common at the place and time. All of this was later born out by the fact that the recovered items were all very small, portable and personal. Such items as combs, brushes, coins, a brass mirror, and ornamental costume jewelry were present and were common as payment or currency in the particular times.

I would now like to focus on the long held consensus that have surrounded, certain accounts from history, but which have proven to be not necessarily as they have always been handed down to us in our history books from our formative years in school. As I mentioned earlier, my quest for truth began early. Along that twisted and sometimes rough path I hit many roadblocks which yielded some uncertainty. Was what I was reading, seeing, or being taught the real story or even the whole story?

One of these road blocks was my journey with the Roman

Catholic Church and it's indoctrination by way of catechism classes lasting nearly nine months called CCD (Confraternity of Christian Doctrine). Nowhere in any of the material provided did they include any church history or even a hint as to why there was this huge divide between Catholics and "Protestants". I never heard the word Reformation even once. And, of course I understand now it would not bode well for "The Church" to teach about those aspects of church history or about their nemesis Martin Luther and his 95 theses. I'm certainly not going to cover all that here, but suffice to say that everyone who claims to follow Christ ought to avail themselves of the study of church history (Christian history).

Over the years I have found that I can't accept every single thing at face value. After that experience with the Roman Catholic Church and her trusted leaders and teachers (the priests I inquired of), I became very leery and determined, with focused diligence, to find my own answers. Just because someone hales from the elite Universities, has tenure, and a long list of letters behind their name, does not mean they have the defacto answers. Sometimes we must accept that we may never have all the answers, but then, we who are of faith are used to that.

Some answers are not really the right ones even though sincerely given. One example from my early childhood was concerning dinosaurs. What child is not enthralled with dinosaurs? I had this book with awe inspiring pictures and facts about some of the more popular dinosaurs from the past. OK, let's look at what I just said, with attention given to the word "facts". I must use that term very loosely as did the author of my book.

This author was a respected Paleontologist who had Doctor in front of his name and a lot of letters after. According to this Doctor he was presenting facts. One of those facts which I carried with me for years was that the dinosaurs were all cold blooded reptiles. This was the impression left me and countless other children. Years later I learned from my own studies (I just love all the sciences) that the global landscape was populated with all kinds of animals and not all dinosaurs were reptilian, but some, if not most, were closer to birds possessing bird-like qualities such as feathers and soft bones, etc.

Another prime example is from Astronomy. I'm sure most all of us remember being taught that our solar system was made up of "nine major planets in increasing distance from the Sun, MERCURY, VENUS, EARTH, MARS, JUPITER, SATURN, URANUS, NEPTUNE, and PLUTO"[1] This is no longer the fact! In 2006 The IAU changed Pluto's status to that of "dwarf planet"[2]. Pluto was demoted from planet to a Kuyper Belt Object or Plutoid.

We are all familiar with the old song, "in 1492 Columbus sailed the ocean blue" and discovered America right? That's what most of us grew up learning in our history books at school.

Columbus actually landed at San Salvador Island, Cuba.

I could go on and on, but I think you get the point. As to history and what we've always been taught, there seems to exist a lot of gray area; some misconceptions and inaccuracies in the "facts". There seem to be other "versions" of the stories. Who do we believe? Who is Giving us the truth? Who can we trust? All very good questions and ones I intend to answer.

Chapter three individual study/group discussion questions;

Have you ever had a long-held belief about something only to have it turn out to be completely different?

Why do you think there are so many views of Philosophy, History, Science... and yes, even Religion?

Chapter 4

POLITICS: LIONS, TIGERS, AND BEARS...OH MY

"And God looked upon the earth, and, behold, it was corrupt; for all flesh had corrupted his way upon the earth."

"Help, LORD; for the godly man ceaseth; for the faithful fail from among the children of men." (Gen. 6:12 & Psalm 12:1)

"We have been the recipients of the choicest bounties of Heaven. We have preserved, these many years, in peace and prosperity. We have grown in numbers, wealth, and power, as no other nation has ever grown. But we have forgotten God. We have forgotten the gracious hand which preserved us in peace and multiplied and enriched and strengthened us; and we have vainly imagined, in the deceitfulness of our hearts, that all these blessings were produced by some superior wisdom and virtue of our own. Intoxicated with unbroken success, we have become too self-sufficient to feel the necessity of redeeming and preserving grace, too proud to pray to the God that made us! It behooves us, then to humble ourselves before the offended Power, to confess our national sins, and to pray for clemency and forgiveness." (Proclamation appointing a National Fast Day - Washington, D.C., March 30, 1863) Abraham Lincoln

If I had not given due credit to that last quote, there are many in this country who never would have guessed that it came from an actual President of the United States and not from some eloquent pastor type like Dr. Martin Luther King Jr. Not only that, but that it came from over 150 years ago. The political climate, even in President Lincoln's day, was one of chaos and corruption. But, compared to the climate of today's culture, it appears as child's play in comparison. As I mentioned at the beginning, we have seen an obvious decline in the moral standards and traditional values of this once great nation. -- OK! I won't' put the last nail in that coffin just yet; and to be fair, we are still a great nation, but, and I hate to say it, I believe there is a terminal cancer eating away at the pillars and foundations which have made us great. Based on Abraham Lincoln's quote I think he felt the same.

The Founding Fathers were well aware that governmental powers were not meant to be vested in one man, or in one political group. Judaeo-Christian principles contributed to the founder's collective notion of separation of powers. As a result they established three branches of government - the Judicial, Legislative, and the Executive branches (their inspiration was that God is our ultimate Judge, giver of Law, and King-from Isaiah 33:22). The ingenious Federal system was also set up to be representative of all of the States - That, my friend, is the "we the people" part. As can be seen, the founders constructed a system of checks and balances that would protect against a direct democracy and which said, "the voice of the people is the voice of God"(James Madison). Now wait a minute. Why would a founder make a statement like that? Simply because the expectation was that America was founded as a Christian nation with a citizenry of God-fearing voters (not God hating ones) well in the majority by at least a 90% margin. The same holds for true for the founders themselves.

They wove the colonies into a republic where the will of the people is sifted through elected representatives who were intended, quite staunchly, to be persons of virtue and who exhibited a concern for the common good and who could rise above petty squabbles and particular fanciful causes of the day to work together (that means bipartisan) to achieve a wonderful balance.

For better than two centuries, the hard won republic known as America has given the world a beautiful example of the way "the laws of Nature and Nature's God" (Biblical Principles) can preserve, sustain, order, and secure liberty for all. Yet, for all of modern society's knowledge and advanced technology, those founding principles are consistently eroding from the winds and waves of an aggressive force known as Secularism (& Humanism). The very fabric of our nation is under attack and the prognosis is not good at all!

One might ask, "What does SECULAR even mean?" Secular-

1. worldly rather than spiritual 2. not related to religion[1]. Websters: not sacred or ecclesiastical - non-religious [civil, of or belonging to government or the people][2]. We can't define that and not define Secularism - this is the philosophy which says that humanity's betterment is best achieved without reference to God or religion. It is based on assumption that materialism is the be all and end all for the average man; thus it is man centric (hence Humanism), temporal, and greedily materialistic[3].

Secular-Humanism then, is a multifaceted philosophical trend much like Communism or Marxism and has many components like Post-modernism, Liberalism, and Progressivism all of which seek to remove God, Jesus Christ, and the Bible from all areas of the public sector. Quite the opposite of what the founders had intended! Bill O'Reilly put it this way, "The brilliant men who forged the Constitution understood that Americans should have the opportunity to pursue happiness without government interference. They also believed, for both moral and practical reasons, that the greater good must always take precedence over individual selfishness... To that end the founders acknowledged that religion and spirituality could be effective bulwarks against anarchy and crime, so they encouraged a society 'under God.' But now all of that has been rejected by the secular-progressive movement (secular-humanism), which holds that widespread belief in a higher power is one of the causes of social injustice... and 'under God' is now ... 'under legal review' "[4]

The Secular-Humanism agenda is clung to most ardently by avid liberals and even more so for those on the far left, unabashed and unapologetic socialists. It almost seems like conservatism is quickly becoming a bad word in our modern society. The far left leaning agenda is now everywhere. This sinister plot has permeated the majority of the dominant culture. We see it so very plainly in the school systems across this country; in the entertainment, TV, and Movie industry and music industry too; in the books we read and in the news and media outlets especially so. Let's stop right there and put it in park for a bit as we allow the engine to idle on the Media.

In his national bestseller "Conservative Comebacks to Liberal Lies" Gregg Jackson has collected some eyebrow raising facts concerning many liberal talking points which are, in reality, bold face lies. He also shows a very clear liberal bias in the media.

Journalists and the mainstream media have always claimed to be unbiased, balanced, and fair in their reporting. But the secret has been shattered. Though many have known as far back as the 50's & 60's, the world has now been awakened to the far left leanings of the major networks (ABC, NBC, CBS, CNN) and of the major metropolitan newspapers like the ultra far left New York Times, The Washington Post, Chicago Tribune, and on, and on. Liberals have long used their friends in the mainstream media to influence public policy by slanting news coverage to support their ideologies (abortion on demand, LGBTQ issues, etc.). Jackson lists numerous poll results from the 90's and early 2000's showing unmistakable liberal bias. He even included this from Peter Jennings ABC News anchor, "Historically in the media, it has been more of a liberal persuasion for many years. It has taken us a long time -- too long in my view -- to have vigorous conservative voices heard as widely in the media as they are now"[5&6].

Even when you consider those conservative voices like Rush Limbaugh, Glenn Beck, Sean Hannity, Michael Savage, Sheryl Atkison, etc., etc. They are still only a drop in the proverbial bucket of liberal bias. In just the last 3 - 4 years (since 2015) we have seen some eye opening events come to the fore allowing all of America to see just how slanted the left is. For example: The 2016 Presidential Election was one of those events which will be indelibly written on the pages of history as "The Big Surprise." One key phrase which has garnered endless play, even by the left (who it was intended to denigrate), which served to put the spotlight on obvious liberal bias, is when Presidential candidate Donald Trump characterized the mainstream media (especially CNN) as "Fake News" ! All media, print and broadcast have relentlessly dogged him ever since. And ... speaking of "Fake News"...

> You know the the politically correct landscape is crazy when the CEO of the social media juggernaut Facebook, Mark Zuckerberg, is summoned before Congress to testify in hearings on Capital Hill. WIRED Magazine ran an article about this story in their March 2018 edition. What follows is edited for length and is not an exact quote but is paraphrased for brevity.

The recent fake news flurry was confirmed when outside analysts found incriminating evidence of Russian bought ads which gave rise to Congressional hearings. The normally reclusive founder of Facebook came out into the light in a very public way. He was visibly shaken by the nefarious Russian antics perpetrated within the public social media site's framework.

Zuckerberg appeared very humble as the Congressional hearings commenced. The committee members grilled him and seemed unrelenting. They wanted to know how a foreign Power could possibly wreak the havoc they did with his own creation as their weapon delivering just enough false propaganda so as to turn 3000 Russian bought ads into 340 million (I seriously question this number) echoes in the form of re-posts on the social media website.

[What's the point? Well, I'm glad you asked.] Though Zuckerberg's politics (he's one of those far left leaning liberals) do not necessarily favor conservatives, and most especially Donald Trump, he was still angry at how someone could so deftly manipulate people and information via his creation which was made as he put it, "to better our world". At about the same time a former employee blew the whistle on internal, tightly held, policies which regularly squelched conservative views and news. This all considered, dealt quite a blow and caused much soul searching on the part of Facebook's embattled leader. The Trump campaign had proven an effective stimulus for a new breed of scammers pumping out massively viral, yet entirely fake news stories. Zuckerberg's indignation toward them (the Russians) turned inward in an awkward twist when he was informed, as were the rest of us as the story broke, as to the conservative squelching (which went wildly public). This was yet another thorn in the flesh for Zuckerberg. ~ In February 2017 he published a 5,700 word corporate manifesto which began with the question, "Are we building the world we all want?" This preceded sweeping changes at Facebook designed to revamp, not just the company's image, but their purpose and their responsibility to that global community they sought to build and keep.[7]

The author of this WIRED Magazine article is an obvious liberal, but I will say more moderate than most despite his support for poor Mark Zuckerberg. The events did have some sort of impact on the bedraggled social media site founder. It was very reminiscent of a Jerry Maguire moment with the corporate manifesto having been delivered to every single Facebook employee. My bet is that Zuckerberg felt like quite the hypocrite after all that transpired. It is a rare sight indeed to witness, in a very public way, actual remorse and regret from the liberal left.

If not for "real" Christians (what some call evangelicals), conservatives, true patriots, genuine republicans, and yes, even some moderates, we as a modern American society would not look at all like America the beautiful, but we would be the Unified Socialist States Re-born (USSR)! I know that sounds crazy, but it is not outside the realm of possibility for the extreme left! Of those conservative voices mentioned earlier, Janie B. Chaney of World Magazine is one in a terrific group at that publication. In one of her articles she said something I just had to jot down and save, "In the United States, the game of Politics, always tinged with an aspect of hooliganism, {likewise}, threatens to turn deadly."[8] [remember the Democrat -vs- Republican baseball game shooting?]

George Washington summed up my point quite well when he said, "Reason and experience both forbid us to expect that national morality can prevail in the exclusion of religious principle." What a brilliant man he was! Secular-Humanists, liberals, (especially the far left), evolutionist as well as other modern "scientists" all want the same thing. They want to kick God and Christian principles and good wholesome traditional values out of the public square. Why? Because, if there is put before them such a standard of decent and moral behavior with God at the center of it all, well then, that would mean a complete fundamental shift in personal responsibility and beliefs from a Man centered and selfish mindset (WORLDVIEW) to a God centered one -- a Christian one.

How else can one explain how a government could go so wrong as to legalize murder for personal convenience calling it "Reproductive Rights" or hiding it behind the banner of women's healthcare? Also, how could that same government so thoroughly wreck the Family as to completely redefine marriage and allow same sex unions which are still an "abomination" today? These folks, and to be fair it is usually the far left, have been relatively successful at replacing the pure and religious principles which our founding fathers built into the fabric of this nation, and have replaced them with "secular-humanism", "multiculturalism", "diversity & acceptance", "social justice", "moral relativism", "political correctness", and, let's not forget, "cradle to grave welfare." Their motives and methods are right out of the Marxist playbook and are meant to put this country on the fast-track to socialism. Politics is indeed a sinister enterprise. Thank God for the fact that there yet exists a tattered remnant of the original checks and balances acting as a strained and buckling dam to stem the torrent of the liberal left. Let's all pray that dam holds!

Chapter Four individual study/group disscusion questions

Before reading this chapter, did you know what, "Secular," meant? Does its meaning change how you think about our society and government?

Have you personally noticed the liberal slant in education, Entertainment and media? Why do you think this is?

Why has the liberal, (Secular,) agenda been so successful? What do you think is the solution to stem the tide?

Chapter 5

A BIBLICAL MANIFESTO DEBUNKING EVOLUTION

"In the beginning God created the heaven and the earth." (Genesis 1: 1)

One place one would expect to find truth is in the Sciences. After all, the word "science" means: "knowledge covering general truths or the operation of general laws especially as obtained and tested through the scientific method."[1] What I (and many others) call "pure" science is that which investigates, observes, and formulates a hypothesis (educated guess), but can't give a definitive conclusion without full analysis, further testing, observation of results and retesting until a final conclusion, if possible, can be made based on concrete evidence resulting from the scientific method. Much of what I have witnessed from the scientific community since I began my own quest for the truth is not, by any means, pure science. I have witnessed theories put forth as fact. Guesswork collected from a consensus and called defacto truth. Did you know that in Columbus' day the consensus of the scientific community was that the world was flat?

I have chosen to discuss evolution as it is one of the fist things one is taught (as fact) in school under the banner of science. There existed no other option in the textbooks that I can recall. As I had mentioned, science was always my favorite subject and this exposure to evolution was my first venture in the sciences where I had to stop and say to myself, "Hey, somebody's lying!" The Bible says, "In the beginning God created the heaven and the earth." (Gen. 1:1 KJV) The textbook in my elementary school said man (whom the Bible says was created by God on the sixth {literal days} day) was, eons ago, a one celled protozoa in some slime pool, then developed by means of evolution slowly over millions upon millions of years in a gradual process. First to reptile (from a fish), to a bird, to a mammal, and finally to man. There was also this thing that started it all called The Big Bang (how does nothing go "bang"?).

As kids we were told to trust those learned scientists who have studied for years and years and have come together in agreement assuring us all along that their conclusions are to be taken as gospel, but wait a minute. Didn't I read that all of these ideas they were trying to sell me as facts are actually a theory, a hypothesis? An educated guess is still a guess. This sort of guesswork does not meet the definition of pure science! So why do they proffer it as the truth if it is only guesswork? Then, on the other side you have the pastors, preachers, and other religious leaders telling one to trust God and His word revealed to us in the Bible. Who is right? Just hang in there with me and I will answer that. The dictionary says of evolution -- "a theory that the various kinds of plants and animals are descended from other kinds that lived in earlier times and that the differences are due to inherited changes that occurred over many generations."[2]

In his youth Charles Darwin, the father of evolutionary theory, and author of "The Origin of Species by Natural Selection" (1856), was raised a Christian; his father wanted him to be a minister. The young Darwin actually believed the Bible, and a little later as a young man wrote letters quoting the Bible. As he moved headlong into adulthood he turned to the sciences eventually rejecting the Bible and God saying, "I believe there never has been any revelation." Much later in life, he even admitted in a letter to a friend that his ideas about the origins and decent of man "seemed more and more to be weakening and losing feasibility." One of his final comments in this regard was, "I must be content to remain an agnostic, the beginning of all things is a mystery insolvable by us."

At this point I must mention the compromising idea called Theistic Evolution which says that God set things into motion which then continued in this thing called evolution and that the old Genesis story did not mean literal days. There was a huge gap between Genesis 1:1 and 1:2 of millions of years.(This is called the Gap Theory)[3] There is no verse in Scripture which explicitly talks of an earlier creation or of some earlier judgment/wrath against the earth. This Gap Theory is not even in the realm of possibility based on all of Scripture.

Evolutionary theory has remarkably fit hand-in-glove with the other sciences such as Geology and Stellar Cosmology which also claim the idea of millions and millions of years and origins completely devoid of God. This is the crux of the problem. Who do you believe? With all the crazy and outlandish "theories" out there where this scientist says this, and that scientist says that, which contradicts not just each other, but the Bible too, we are left to sort through the mess. Then we must decide which makes more sense. William Jennings Bryan once said, "I had rather begin with God and reason down, than to start with a piece of dirt and reason up."

Frankly, I'm astounded that very intelligent men would even side with the absolute silliness of the whole evolutionary mindset! The snap argument most proponents of evolution make is in regard to the many scientific dating methods that are so "accurate". What the scientists don't share with each other or with the general public is the many thousands of errors and vast discrepancies found in all of the dating methods. There are, even by geological standards, many influences, be they chemical, pressure, leaching, deluge, etc., which can drastically affect results of a particular sample. One of the lunar astronauts had a great idea to test the moon rocks.

The excitement in the scientific community at the opportunity to test the moon rocks was short lived. The idea was that these samples did not have the many negative earth-like influences of rain, wind, and pressures. Across the board the age spread came back from 2 million to over 28 billion years! With so much contradictory information, ideas, and results, who is right? Now that's a great question. I'll get to that in a bit, but first allow me elaborate on this Darwin fella who so many have, at least for the last century, clung to as a brilliant man with brilliant ideas.

Darwin had some ideas that would surprise you. He thought about and wrote about man's mind and how it was, "clearly superior to woman's." [if he lived in our day and age he'd be laughed right out of the room] Here is his explanation: He said that when our ancestors were yet in the animal stage (that is pure Darwinism) the males fought for the females. In their quest for superior mates the more excellent and stronger males also developed increased brain power. [when I see young men chasing after women today, I just don't see the correlation]. According to Darwin this increased brain capacity did not descend to both males and females, just the males! Is this not ludicrous? Well there is more... How did mankind lose all that thick body hair? (remember the so-called apelike man vs modern man). By the females consistently selecting toward a preference of less and less hair on their men! This is the guy the evolutionists and naturalists hung their hats on for so many years. The same man who, at the end of his life, said there really wasn't much to his ideas.

Why would otherwise really intelligent people put so much stock in Darwinian ideas? Like Lucifer, man wants to usurp the authority of God and be the god of his own life (this is why we are called depraved [reprobate]; not my word, God's). This is the same as a the secular humanist and modernist liberals who have foisted God from any claim on their lives and from the public sectors. Even many so-called Christians cry along with the dominant culture, "I am the master of my own fate; the captain of my own destiny." What we are left with is a presupposition that is anti-God, anti-supernatural, and anti-religion. Just as the founding of our country presupposed Almighty God, but has in the last century been allowed to tie Him up and toss Him into a corner, so these folks have taken the only source of pure truth away and now hold to their own version.

"For the wrath of God is revealed from heaven against all ungodliness and unrighteousness of men, who hold the truth in unrighteousness." (Rom.1:18) And so here it is, that which Paul told the Romans, "For the invisible things of him from the creation of the world are clearly seen, being understood by the things that are made, even His eternal power and Godhead; so that they (the unbelievers) are without excuse."(Rom.1:20) But we must also look at the very next verse which makes all of this abundantly clear, "For although they knew God they did not honor Him as God or give thanks to him, but they became futile in their thinking and their senseless minds were darkened." (Rom. 1:21 RSV) Now we should not really be surprised. When you know deep down inside, in the place where self-talk occurs, that God IS [just as he said, "I Am"] and you choose to ignore Him, undercut Him, and go your own way, that is the "unrighteousness of men" and puts man under the wrath of God.

What many folks do not realize is that William Jennings Bryan was not just a very keen lawyer and statesman, but he was a very gifted Christian apologist. In a piece called The Bible or Evolution he exposes evolution without even leaving the first chapter of Genesis. Dr. Bryan showed three simple verses which completely obliterate the sham we have allowed to be perpetrated as modern science and worse, have allowed it to be spoon fed to our school children for nearly a century. He began at the perfect starting place (Gen. 1:1 KJV), "In the beginning God created the heaven and the earth." The first four words really sum it all up pretty good "In the beginning God..." He is the source - not some Big Bang - well, maybe that was God clapping His hands together as he got started. Man would have us believe that the universe, the world, and all the life that exists because, as Dr. Francis Schaeffer put it, "matter or energy which has existed forever in some form, shaped into its present complexity by pure chance."

The second verse that Bryan focused on was Genesis 1:24, "And God said, let the earth bring forth the living creatures after his kind, cattle, and creeping thing, and beast of the earth after his kind: and it was so." Bryan rightly pointed out that Moses was no scientist and the Bible was never meant to be a book of science; yet right there in the well attested ancient text of 3500 years ago, is the most important scientific fact of all time regarding all life on earth. Even folks without a college or university degree can see out of their window that there are laws that govern life and matter. For life to propagate upon the earth it must be reproduced and that according to the law set by God according to "kind". No living thing in either the animal or vegetable kingdoms has ever violated that law. Every form of life is reproduced according to its own unique "kind"; including man. Oh, man has tried to play God with genetics and cloning and such, but, at best, all he's ever been able to do is cause variation and sterile hybrids which always revert back to original DNA base code authored by God himself. The third and final verse that Bryan focused on was Gen. 1:26, "And God said, let us make man in our image, after our likeness: and let them have dominion over the fish of the sea, and over the fowl of the air, and over the cattle, and over all the earth, and over every creeping thing that creepeth upon the earth."

We could well stay right there and write thousands of books ~ Oh, wait, the philosophers and thinkers have already done that and they were and are still confused with no solution of their own apart from divine fiat. It would be an easy thing to just go on and on about how man was made quite a bit different from the other "creatures". I could fill page after page about dualism (which, in religion, says man in essence is both physical and mind {spirit}) and no other animal thinks, ponders, and creates as man, but I'll keep the focus, as Bryan did, on two key words from the verse that strike at the heart of who we are and why we are here: "image" and "likeness".

We already know that without help from above man can't ever fully grasp the reason for his own existence. I used to shake my fist at God and say, "I never asked to be born!" Little did I know that I was on to something with that statement. Man has no say in how, when, or where he will be born; not what race, social standing, or country. With this in mind it becomes easy to see why evolutionists and humanists default to pure chance, but this is not in accord with what God said. When you behold all that God created; the beauty, the splendor, the absolute perfection and precision, then you see Him place man in dominion over all the earth. This was right after making man in His own "image" and after His "likeness". And, as I said, there has been, and yet could be, much discussion about the meaning of those two words, but I like how Dr. Wayne Grudem put it in his "Systematic Theology", "When we realize that the Hebrew words for "image" and "likeness" simply informed the original readers that man was like God, and would in many ways represent God, much of the controversy over the meaning of "image of God" is seen to be a search for too narrow and too specific a meaning.

When scripture reports that God said, 'let us make man in our image, after our likeness' (Gen 1:26), it simply would have meant to the original readers, 'let us make man to be like us, and to represent us.' Because image and likeness had these meanings, Scripture does not need to say something like, ~ The fact that man is in the image of God means that man is like God in the following ways: intellectual ability, moral purity, spiritual nature, dominion over the earth, creativity, ability to make ethical choices, and immortality [or some similar statement].

Such an explanation is unnecessary. . . no such list could do justice to the subject."[5]

Now I will give Dr. William Jennings Bryan's summary of the three verses in his piece on The Bible and Evolution: "Here are the three verses; the first one, Gen 1:1, gives us the origin of life; the second one, Gen 1:24, gives us the law governing life's continuity; and the third one, Gen 1:26, gives us the explanation of man's presence here. You cannot find this anywhere else.

Search your libraries, read your books, and among all the things that man has said, you cannot collect from them all anything equal in importance to man to that which you find in three verses of one chapter of Genesis and we have all the rest of the Bible besides."

When I was in my 20's and 30's I used to be a Theistic Evolutionist. I did not know the Bible then. Even before my first full year of intense and diligent study of the Bible, I was converted into a fully convinced and sold out creationist. I still know some folks who are very intelligent, say they are Christians, and believe in Theistic Evolution. I am here to tell you they are not Christian in their doctrine! Noted Pastor, preacher and editor Dr. John R. Rice said this, "A man may be converted and still be ignorant. A man may be converted and still not learn Bible Doctrine [this is true of over 70% of mainstream Christians. To the shame of Christian Educators]. A man may have trusted Jesus Christ and still swallow things ignorantly . . . But the plain truth is that doctrinally and every other way the theory of evolution is against the Bible and against Christianity. They are contradictory."

Please remember this, especially the next time you are watching the Discovery Channel or some other animal or nature program, that evolution is (and always has been) a guess. Its foundation, like a house of cards in a stiff breeze, is all about supposition -- a preconceived world and universe without God and without the Bible. There is no real and conclusive scientific evidence that proves evolution is a fact! --- I had asked earlier, who do we believe? we must make a choice. It really comes down to whether you trust all those many voices, books, lectures, films, and textbooks (which can be very confusing to say the least). There is no tangible or absolute evidence to put trust in and, as a matter of fact, most evolutionists admit that there is no readily visible change in species today. Did it just stop? OK, maybe it was that one law that took over. The second law of thermodynamics which states that, if left to themselves all things tend to greater randomness and decay. (things just get old and wear out). That's what stopped the changes right? [no, its what clipped evolution's wings]. The fact is, very few even casually mention Darwin's name these days.

For the Christian it is as simple as those three verses in Genesis. God has more than proven himself. His unique signature is everywhere in His creation. God is to be trusted -- not man

Paul said, "let God be true and every man a liar" (Rm 3:4). The

Bible is to be trusted as it is the word of our omnipotent God who cannot lie. It proves that evolution is indeed a bunch of monkey business. The theory has been shut down from one end of the spectrum to the other while God's word "is able to make one wise unto salvation."

Chapter Five individual study/group discusion questions

Why do you think Evolution and other "theories" are put forth as fact?

What does it mean to you that man was made in the "image" and "Likeness" of God?

What goes through your mind when Science and nature shows say things like; "Dogs are descended from Wolves."and the "Universe is billions and billions of years old?"

PART II

Chapter 6

CREEDS, CONFESSIONS, AND CATECHISMS

"Christianity fails today because it isn't being explained. It isn't being explained because people don't know what they believe. They don't know why they believe it and they don't know why it matters." Charles Colson

From the very beginning of this work I have made mention of my own personal quest for truth. The journey has been one of adventure, hope, heartache and then ... home. I say home because, of all of my travels abroad to exotic places like France, Greece, Italy, and even Russia, its still always great to get back home; where everything is comfortable, cozy, and familiar. Speaking of home; it should be fairly obvious by now where I believe the absolute source of truth is. In case you missed it somehow -- God and his revelation to man in His word, The Bible. Francis Schaeffer put it this way: "Many Christians do not mean what I mean when I say Christianity is true, or Truth . . . When I say Christianity is true I mean it is true to total reality -- the total of what is, beginning with the central reality, the objective existence of the personal-infinite God. Christianity is not just a series of truths but TRUTH -- Truth about all of reality."[1]

Jesus put it best when He said, "I am the way, the truth, and the life . . ." but He went on, "no man cometh unto the Father, but by me."(John 14:6) I really don't know how it could be any clearer than that. Jesus of Nazareth, Messiah -- our Christ -- God come in the flesh -- is TRUTH! But, He is also the way, and the life. The importance of that very statement can't be grasped in simple academic terms. Sure, you can take it in, acknowledge it, and even agree with it, but that is not the totality of it. Truths like this must be grasped by a spiritual man. What does that mean; "Spiritual man"?

Here is the disconnect that almost no one speaks on! You have two types out there, the natural man and the spiritual man. Jesus dealt with this very thing in His nighttime meeting with a highly regarded religious man of the Pharisees, Nicodemus. When He told Nicodemus that a man must be "born again" that threw this Pharisee for a loop. That is because Nicodemus is earthly in his understanding -- natural in his thinking. The man standing before him (Jesus) is unlike any other man ever born of woman. He is the God-man. He is all God (heavenly being) and yet all man (earthly being) and is trying to get Nicodemus to understand what "born again" really means (the literal translation is born from above).This second birth or New birth is indeed from above by way of the Holy Spirit (thereby making this whole concept spiritual in nature) giving life to those dead in trespasses and sins thus allowing one to see and enter the Kingdom of God.

As the conversation progressed Jesus scolded Nicodemus a bit for not catching on to "heavenly things". I'm not going to go real deep into this just now (read John 3), but rest assured a much thicker book could well be written on this subject alone. I do like how Paul put it in His first letter to the Corinthians, "but the natural man receiveth not the things of the Spirit of God: for they are foolishness unto him: neither can he know them, because they are spiritually discerned." (I Cor. 2:14) This right here is the disconnect I mentioned. Obviously Jesus knew He was not wasting his time on Nicodemus -- that he would eventually grasp the spiritual (heavenly) things. Some, like

Judas Iscariot, never get it. As Christians we all face it (if we are soul winners) all the time -- people who just don't get it. Then there are those who can grasp the spiritual somewhat, but not all of it. This is what motivated Nicodemus to seek out this Jesus of Nazareth fella. He was a man in transition. He just knew that there was more than meets the eye in this "Teacher come from God." Nicodemus was a man in search of the truth. He would never be able to see or grasp the full truth without this second or re-birth (more on that later).

Whenever I teach / preach, I never assume that the whole audience is "Christian" or as an old Southern Baptist preacher put it, "Born again and blood bought." There is a difference -- just look at Peter and then Judas. With that said I'll move on with the understanding that as I unfold the story behind creeds, confessions, and catechisms and then cover the core of Christian doctrine about God, Jesus Christ, The Holy Spirit, etc., etc., there will be some who just don't get it. This is just an unfortunate fact. But then this book is not really written for them. I am, however, going to cover that very Gospel that Jesus shared with a very astute "religious" man -- because one never knows who is right at the verge of eternal life as Nicodemus was. We never know whom God has chosen and predestined as His elect on any given day whether we share the gospel one on one, or preach to an arena full, or write to stir the hearts of many, or just one -- we just don't know.

My experience with the Roman Catholic Church in my teens was not all bad. There were aspects of that faith that I still, to this day, admire and remember fondly. There was a certain awe and reverence whenever I entered a Catholic Church. I just knew God was there. I am still moved by the beauty of the statues, stained glass, and breathtaking architecture of some of the older churches and cathedrals. The robes, the pews with their kneelers, the altar, the candles, and the sign of the cross when entering. I was particularly moved by the responsive readings we would all recite as part of the Mass.

My favorites were the Nicene creed and the shorter more personal Apostle's creed. The apostle's creed was a shorter version and began a little differently. As a congregation, reciting the Nicene creed began with, "We believe…" But the Apostle's creed, often taught in basic core catechism, began, "I believe…" This is exactly where our English word creed came from. The Latin word credo means "I believe". I have seen where some cast a negative air upon creeds and confessions (and even doctrine). Some just do not want to be responsible to a standard. They want freedom from restraint. They want something fluid and changeable. God and His word are not like that! Jesus put the Devil right in his place when, in the wilderness temptation story, Jesus was at the end of a 40 day fast and was very hungry. The devil challenged Jesus to make stones into bread ,but Jesus told him, "man shall not live by bread alone, but by every word that proceedeth out of the mouth of God. (Matt 4:3-4) Jesus was quoting Deuteronomy 8:3 where Moses was reminding Israel of that same unchangeable precept.

As Christians we understand God gave us Scripture as our only infallible guide for faith and life. It stands to reason then that it (the Bible) is our unwavering standard for our beliefs. As Paul told the up and coming pastor Timothy, "All scripture is given by inspiration of God, and is profitable for doctrine, for reproof, for correction, for instruction in righteousness…"(II Tim 3:16)

OK. Why proclaim what the Bible already teaches? Why do we need a creed anyway?

Now that is a great question and so I'll jump right in and answer it. Just as the devil tempted Jesus and even used scripture to do so, so he plays by the same rules today. He works through agents to sew division, discord and above all error (heresy). Let's go back in time a bit and see the very first creed of the people of God. A creed recited by the assembled people who gathered for each of the four main festivals each year celebrated in Jerusalem. On Passover, Pentecost, Day of Atonement, and Feast of Tabernacles, the "Shema" was repeated among the assembled: "Hear, O Israel: The Lord our God is one Lord: And thou shalt love the Lord thy God with all thine heart, and with all thy soul, and with all thy might."(Deut. 6:4-5) The word "Shema" is a transliteration of Hebrew meaning "hear" as the

A Christian Manifesto for the Twenty-first Century

basic statement of the Jewish Law. The Shema became for the people of God a confession of faith by which they acknowledged the one true God and His commandments for them.

The very first Christians were Jews who were already steeped in the tradition of reciting a creed. They were familiar with a statement of belief and so it only made sense to have one for this [new] faith. They already believed in God and knew that Jesus was the Messiah promised by scripture. R. C. Sproul once said of creeds, "Creedal statements are an attempt to show a coherent and unified understanding of the whole scope of scripture."[1a] Creeds have been developed and adhered to because they are a reflection of fundamental Bible doctrines. Creeds exist because they affirm and reflect truth -- not produce it. Truth is not created by man and can only be learned from God. Many have tried to forge their own versions of doctrine and/or truth.

There are names from history that will be forever etched in

infamy. Such was Arius who was a popular elder/ overseer in the Alexandrian Church. His views stood in stark opposition to the Bible. Such as: "God was not always Father - the Word of God did not always exist...but came into being from things that did not exist making the Son a created being - the Word does not either know or see the Father perfectly; He does not even know his own nature as it really is."[2] Arius believed that the Son was not divine, and that he was a creature like any other. It boggles the brain as to how he could have come to such far out conclusions, but not only did he think them, but wrote about them and taught them as doctrine. He was condemned by a council of bishops convened by Alexander Bishop of Alexandria. Arius appealed to Emperor Constantine who then called for a world council of 318 bishops from all over the known world to settle the matter once and for all. They met in Nicaea in 325 A.D. Arius came into the session with only minimal support from 17 bishops, but by the end of all testimony and close of the session that support dwindled to just 2. Not only was the official condemnation upheld, but the council decided on a newer more comprehensive statement of faith;

thus we see the birth of The Nicene Creed which is still recited by churches today:

> "We believe in one God, the Father Almighty, Maker of heaven and earth, of all things visible and invisible. and in one Lord Jesus Christ, the only-begotten Son of God, begotten of His Father before all worlds; God of God, Light of Light, very God of very God; begotten, not made, being of one substance with the Father, by whom all things were made; Who, for us men and for our salvation, came down from heaven, and was incarnate by the Holy Spirit of the Virgin Mary, and was made man; and was crucified also for us under Pontius Pilate; He suffered, [died] and was buried; and the third day he rose again according to the scriptures; and ascended into heaven, and is seated at the right hand of the Father; and He shall come again, with glory, to judge both the living and the dead; Whose kingdom shall have no end.
>
> And we believe in the Holy Spirit, the Lord the giver of Life; who proceeds from the Father and the Son; who with the Father and Son together is worshiped and glorified; who spoke by the prophets. And we believe in one Holy catholic and apostolic church. We acknowledge one baptism for the remission of sins; and we look for the resurrection of the dead, and life of the world to come. Amen."

The Nicene creed was endorsed and expanded at the second major council of Constantinople in 381 A. D. This creed clearly states essential Christian doctrines about God the Father, Jesus Christ the Son, and the Holy Spirit, the Church, Salvation, and the Eternal destiny of the redeemed. It was formulated to combat rampant heresy and affirm the authority of scripture over personal opinions. Burk Parsons, Senior Editor of Table Talk Magazine (Ligonier Ministries) said this about creeds: "The creed simply served to reflect and affirm, by way of a clearly stated systematic summary, the unchanging truth of God for the people of God."

We see a lot of creedal statements in the Bible. I earlier shared the Shema, Deut. 6:4-5, but there are actually quite a few dotted throughout scripture. The most common, I think, is John's summary of the gospel in the words of the Lord in John 3:16. The creed probably seen most is the Apostle's Creed which can be traced as far back as the 2nd century;

> "I believe in God the Father Almighty, maker of heaven and earth; And in Jesus Christ, His only-begotten Son, our Lord; who was conceived by the Holy Spirit, born of the virgin Mary; suffered under Pontius Pilate, was crucified, died, and was buried; (He descended into hell) The third day he rose again from the dead; He ascended into heaven; and sits on the right hand of God the Father, Almighty; from thence He shall come to judge the living and the dead. I believe in the Holy Spirit; the holy catholic church; the communion of saints; the forgiveness of sins; the resurrection of the body, and life everlasting. Amen."

The Nicene creed was certainly a major one for the early church. I will mention some others which came about later: The Chalcedonian creed (451 A.D.), The Athanasian creed 4th - 5th century, The 39 articles by the Church of England, The Westminster Confession & Larger and Smaller catechism (a catechism is simply a text or curriculum summarizing the basic doctrines of a particular faith). Those creeds just mentioned are quite old. There have not been any World councils in hundreds of years. What we see now are the likes of: The London Baptist Confession, The Southern Baptist Faith and

Message, and The Chicago statement on Biblical Inerrancy. Like the Chicago Statement, most creeds today (although that word is rarely used today) reflect the distinctives of their particular denomination.

This very fact is part of the motivation behind this work. I believe Jesus would be [is] very displeased with the division, sectarianism, and denominational-ism in the Church universal today!

As Christians and not simply Baptists, Methodists, Pentecostals, or Lutherans, etc., etc. we all must understand our common faith [core Christian doctrine]. I believe, as did thousands of Spirit led Christians before me, that the Nicene Creed and The Apostle's Creed both embody what all true Christians believe. I am certainly not naive to the fact that there exist differences within the Church universal on various matters such as music, church government, worship styles, Spiritual gifts, etc., etc., but when you look closely at the two main early creeds of Christendom, here included, you will find much in the way of doctrinal agreement among the plethora of "denominations".

This helps us to "all speak the same thing" and "be perfectly joined together in the same mind ." (1 Cor. 1:10). These creeds along with the "love shed abroad in our hearts by the Holy Spirit" (Rom.8:5 KJV) is the glue that holds us in unity, grounded in essential matters such as Salvation and able to show some liberty (latitude) in non-essential matters which do not affect the fundamental doctrines of the Christian Faith. We contribute to that unity by our own affirmations, confessions, and defense of the doctrines so error can't get a foothold.

My goal in presenting the included foundational creeds is to show where the Church laid out these statements as a guide for us all to believe, to confess, to live by, and to proclaim as unchanging doctrines which unite us all in our savior Jesus Christ. With all the competing voices out there and rampant error around every corner, it is an even greater imperative in this day and age (the last of the last days) to know what we believe and why! The creeds help reflect back to us the answers to the what and the why and equip us, "to earnestly contend for the faith which was once for all delivered to the saints" (Jude 3b KJV). Keep in mind what Paul told Timothy, "Preach the word; be instant (prepared) in season, out of season; reprove, rebuke, exhort with all long suffering and doctrine. For the time will come when they will not endure sound doctrine; but after their own lusts shall they heap to themselves teachers, having itching ears; And they shall turn away their ears from the truth, and shall be turned unto fables."

Does this not sound very familiar?

Chapter six individual study/group disscusion questions

Before having read this chapter, did you realize the place Creeds held in the Christian faith?

Why is a creed important in this world today? Do you know the Apostles Creed? Would you want to be able to recite it?

Have you ever experienced a church service that was very different than what you are use to?

Chapter 7

GOD: TO BELIEVE OR NOT TO BELIEVE

"Look unto me, and be ye saved, all the ends of the earth: for I am God, and there is no other" (Is 45:22).

As a curious and inquisitive kid I never really doubted the existence of God. As one with a scientifically inclined mind, I saw order, symmetry (the beautiful mathematics of nature), cohesion, symbiotic mastery, perfection, etc. I could go on and on for a good while with such evidence. There was no doubt in my mind that an all powerful being (Spirit) did all this {The heaven and the earth}. Then, a little later I was a 7 - 8 year old kid whose mom sent him out every Sunday morning to catch that little blue church bus to go learn about God and Jesus at a little country church. I am so glad she did that. There was a sort of confirmation in it. What my eyes saw (in creation) met with the explanation of how it all got here. "In the beginning God created the heaven and the earth"(Gen 1:1).The first 10 words in the Bible -- God's word for mankind leave no doubt and actually don't even try to prove the existence of God -- it just states the simple and plain fact. Where it all gets fouled up is where man comes in with his crazy notions like evolution.

There is in Nature something I like to call The Signature of God.

It is impossible to demonstrate the existence of God for our physical senses because God is not a physical being {God is a Spirit - John 4:24}. But, there is evidence! "The heavens declare the glory of God; and the firmament (skies) sheweth his handiwork" (Ps 19:1). This is what I mean. The very signature of God is left all over His creation. Can anyone really honestly say that the Sun, the rain from heaven, the perfectly timed seasons, and the multitude and variety of seed bearing vegetation are all simply by chance? No! No they can't. When diligent scientists began to unravel the intricate complexities of the DNA molecule they were staring right at God's signature where the ink meets the paper (so to speak). I like what Paul said on this, "For the invisible things of him from the creation of the world are clearly seen, being understood by the things that are made, even his eternal power and Godhead; so that they are without excuse:(Rm 1:20).

A few years after that church bus experience (my first exposure to a real church where I got to go to Sunday School for a bit and later walked that long aisle to go get Jesus in my heart), the Public School system tried to feed me a different story -- one without God! Their version spoke of things like "millions of years" not thousands, and something called "Natural Selection" not after its own kind as well as other "so called" facts.

Something in me said that this just does not add up. They even mentioned, only in passing mind you, that those ideas were part of a "theory", and yet were presented as if there was no other possible explanation. I was just a kid, what did I care at that point? I only wanted to go out for recess.

That was over 40 years ago and even way back then, well before faith and conversion, I decided to take God's word for it. You know, the Bible. Some will complain at this point, " but the Bible was written by men and its just a bunch of myths and far fetched stories." I'll talk more about the Bible later, but right now its all about the Almighty, the Creator of all that is seen and unseen. For most, no matter how hard they may try, it is hard to ignore. So, we evaluate the evidence and if done honestly we see that, all we see in nature proves clearly that God exists and that He is the Omnipotent (all powerful) and Omniscient (all knowing) Creator that Scripture describes Him to be. Therefore, when we believe that God exists, we are basing our belief not on some flimsy hope apart from any solid evidence, but on an overwhelming amount of reliable and tangible evidence all around us in His magnificent "handiwork" -- The Signature of God!

So, what's the problem? Why do some balk at a God / Christ centered way of thinking -- a Christian worldview? In a word -- SIN! If mankind's hearts and minds were not so blinded by sin we could accept the stark truth ever before our eyes. And, unfortunately, some are atheists because they simply do not want religion and its God dictating to them how to speak or act and demanding a change from a irresponsible, selfish, and immoral life to one of selflessness and service to fellow man. Dr. Wayne Grudem, in his Systematic Theology, said this, "... sin causes people to think irrationally."[1] OK, hold it right there. There is that word again - sin. What does that really mean? The Dictionary definition is: "transgression of religious or moral law."[2] The Bible puts a finer point with the literal definition of the Hebrew - abar and Greek - hamartia. It means missing the mark, or coming short of God's divine standard.

We as humans would love to be able to say with confidence that we are rational beings, but we are not! We claim to be against murder and yet we murder the innocent unborn (and even made it legal). We claim to be against sexual immorality and yet we have sex with anybody and everybody we desire (married or not/ same gender or not). We claim to want good health and yet we smoke, drink excessively, and do all sorts of drugs. What on earth is wrong with us? Why do we act contrary to our beliefs. In a

word . . . SIN! More on that later, but for now understand that this is why so many can't accept God or religion and then again why others can accept and are comfortable with organized religion.

This gives them their God and their sin too!

The whole argument for the existence of God has been one that has raged for thousands of years. The study of philosophy especially the arguments for the existence of God can be pretty deep and frankly laborious. It is not without its own interest, but can seem a bit circular after awhile. Thomas Aquinas is considered one of the greatest thinkers (and writers) of his time. He was the main proponent of the first cause argument. This is known as the cosmological argument which is a family of arguments that seek to demonstrate the existence of sufficient reason or first cause of the cosmos. Then we find Anselm of Canterbury who, around 1077 wrote his Monologium which was a very intricate axiological and cosmological argument, but left him unsatisfied. He felt the complexity was simply too much and he yearned for a single argument that, on its own, would prove God exists. He wrote on this and is the Father of the ontological argument. This says that God is "the greatest conceivable being."[3] The ontological argument is based on the science of real existence -- absolute reality as distinct from things as they appear to be. This is only a quick glance of the philosophical treaties on the subject.

Most people do not want to be bothered with the multitude of philosophical arguments so I'll boil it down. There is so much that argues for the existence of God that it becomes irrational not to believe! The scientists and great thinkers base their life's work on observation. Newton did the same as an apple plopped down upon his head and he realized he was experiencing a law -- Gravity. It follows through the centuries that we discovered the law of cause and effect which requires that all things must have a cause -- This demonstrates the existence of God. Everything on His planet, in the sky, and in the vast cosmos clearly shows an undeniable intelligence in its design.

There is intricate precision from the smallest atom to the Awesome red giant star. This level of complexity and organized design can't be simply by chance. The cosmos, our earth, a perfectly favorable for life single star solar system, my existence, and my ability to think and reason must depend on life that does NOT come from nothing, but it requires a reasonable source - a reasonable origin.

Dr. Armand M. Nicholi, distinguished Professor of Philosophy said this, "Within the university students and professors scrutinize every possible aspect of our universe - from the billions of galaxies to subatomic particles, electrons, quarks -- but assiduously (diligently) avoid examining their own lives. In the wider world, we keep hectically busy and fill every free moment of our day with some form of diversion -- work, computers (texting & tweeting), television, movies, radio, magazines, newspapers, sports, alcohol, drugs, parties. Perhaps we distract ourselves because looking at our lives confronts us with our lack of meaning, our unhappiness, and our loneliness . . .and with the brevity of life."[4] Most people come to a point in their lives where they are confronted with a decision. Do I believe {in God}, or don't I? Do I travel down that road of faith or go my own way? Unfortunately, many go the "broad way that leadeth to destruction" (Matt 7:13) Its the easy way - the selfish way. The opposite way is indeed narrow and not at all easy except for one part of it - belief (faith) in the absolute certainty of the existence of God.

As the great C. S. Lewis once said, "God may be known from just two books, scripture and nature." From both we learn of His many attributes. The word or name Elohim, for example, is one of many names for God used in the Old Testament. The interesting thing about this name is the fact that, in Hebrew, it is a Uni-plural noun, meaning more than one (but not in number, yet plurality), and it is used about 2500 times in the Old Testament. There is one place in the Bible where its use is quite revealing.

In Gen 1:26, "And God (Elohim) said, Let us make man in our image, after our likeness . . ." the "us" and "our" are not literary forms denoting royalty. There is no context in the original Hebrew or the Elizabethan style of the KJV. {There is much in this verse, especially concerning the Trinitarian aspect, but that will come in another book} I could surely get long winded here, but my goal is to give a sort of raw crash course on basic Christian Doctrine which is the same for us all from the Roman Catholic in Rio, to the Holiness snake handler in Appalachia, to the fisherman in Hong Kong Harbor who does not know what a denomination is.

One of the foundations of Christian doctrine is the Trinity. Yes, its true that its not explicitly mentioned in the Bible, but just as we can't see God, again, we know he's there. One God in three persons (manifestations). I like the way the Athanasian Creed describes this difficult to explain concept: "So the Father is God; The Son is God; and the Holy Spirit is God. And yet there are not three gods, but one God . . . neither confounding the persons nor dividing the substance." To put it simply, the doctrine of the Trinity (which is essential to orthodox Christian belief) is as follows: God eternally exists as three persons, Father, Son, and Holy Spirit, and each person is fully God, and there is one God.

Many have tried to explain the Trinity with analogies taken from human experience or nature such as an egg or a 3 leaf clover, but all of them fail to capture the full scope of the doctrine. Most attempts fall terribly short of conveying a good understanding. I will try a somewhat different approach in getting you to visualize. Okay, God is eternal -- no beginning and no end. Now visualize a circle. A perfect circle does not have a beginning point, nor end point. Unlike us who are of this earth, God is not bound by time. We are bound to a planet with night and day, seasons, and the Sun which gives us our years. Now think about your own self. You are a three part being -- a three-in-one also.

Body, soul, and spirit. We can't see our soul or spirit, but we know they are there. It is what makes us unique and distinct from others, but it is still a mystery and we can't deny it simply because we don't understand it. The same goes for the Trinity. Okay, now, God is not $1 + 1 + 1 = 3$! He is $1 \times 1 \times 1 = 1$. It is my sincere hope that this was helpful.

My challenge to every Christian is to study such things (as the Trinity) - weigh out what others have said and, of course, use the Bible as the comparative standard to sift such things through. I always tell folks when I teach or preach, "Don't just take my word for it, or another man's -- go to the Bible yourself as the noble Bereans did in Acts 17:11. We are not saved to sit like a bump on a log (pew warmer) useless to the Kingdom of God!

I close this section out with some clear and distinct attributes of God with Holiness as a starting point. This means that, "God is untouched and unstained by the evil in the world - He is pure and perfect."[5] "Who is like unto thee, O LORD, among the gods?

Who is like unto thee, glorious in holiness, fearful in praises, doing wonders?" (Ex 15:11) Keep in mind that this is not an exhaustive list. God is Omniscient which means "knowing all things" - all knowing. He knows everything about everything. He knows our every thought, word, and action. "For His eyes are upon the ways of man, and He seeth all his goings" (Job 34:21). God is Immutable - this means unchanging - He is the same for all time as is His will and His word. "For I am the LORD, I change not . . ."(Mal 3:6). God is Omnipresent - this means He is present everywhere at once in the universe. "The eyes of the LORD are in every place, beholding the evil and the good" (Prov 15:3). God is Omnipotent - this means He is all powerful. God is called "Almighty" because of His incomprehensible power. He parts a sea, stops the Sun, heals the sick, raises the dead, and gives eternal life. "Ah LORD God! Behold thou hast made the heaven and the earth by thy great power ... and there is nothing too hard for thee" (Jer 32:17).

I have shown some basic core evidence for a belief in the existence of God and how His very signature makes it rather senseless not to believe. I have exposed the problem, which has plagued mankind from the beginning, causing most to CHOOSE not to believe -- SIN. I have only dipped a toe into the vast philosophical ocean of views and opinion and briefly touched on a few of man's many distractions and obsessions (idols). I have even thrown around some $25 theological terminology to help describe an indescribable God. "For my thoughts are not your thoughts, neither are my ways your ways, saith the LORD. For as the heavens are higher than the earth, so are my ways higher than your ways, and my thoughts higher than your thoughts" (Is 55:8- 9).

In case you may feel I've overlooked the most important attribute; not to worry. I would never overlook the fact that our God loved the world so much that He gave us His Only begotten Son to die for the sins of the world and so forever solve the sin problem for those who put faith in that atonement! He came to us to die for us so that we could be put back in right relationship with Him with the righteousness of Christ and not our own. Then He left us a piece of Himself (Holy Spirit) who would never leave us or forsake us. That, my friends is a God of Love!

Chapter Seven individual study/group disscusion questions;

Have you always believed in a Natural (by chance) Big Bang kind of Creation or in a Genesis 1:1 Creation?

Give your definition of sin. How does it compare to God's?

What is the most important attribute of God?

CHAPTER 8

THE BIBLE: THE SOURCE OF ALL TRUTH

"Hear the word of the LORD ..." (Is 1:10)

"Thus saith the LORD God . . ." (Joshua 7:13)

"Condemn the truth if you have the heart, but only after you have examined it." – Tertullian 197AD

In the last chapter I covered the reason for everything -- God. I talked about the abundance of evidence in the world and cosmos which, in itself and according to Paul the apostle, leaves man with no excuse not to believe in Him. But God did not leave us with only His obvious signature on nature. He revealed Himself in His word the Bible. Dr. Louis Sperry Chafer wrote, "By this title (God's Word) it is intended to call attention to the claim everywhere present in the Bible that it is God's message to man and not man's message to fellow men . . ." This chapter will be a bit out of sequence from the form I was going to follow of the Apostles Creed as the outline, but it is only logical to begin with God, then cover His revelation to man. The Bible is a collection of books (that's what Bible means). It is the most important of any words ever recorded in the history of the world -- especially in this modern era of chaos, confusion, and abject

A Christian Manifesto for the Twenty-first Century

ignorance of the things of God! The aforementioned is the very reason for this book you are reading.

People want what makes them feel good. Why do you think people flock to motivational speakers like Tony Robbins and to charismatic televangelists like Joel Osteen? Because they make people feel good. They give a false hope -- a human centered hope. "For the time will come when they will not endure sound doctrine; but after their own lusts shall they heap to themselves teachers, having itching ears; and they shall turn away their ears from the truth, and shall be turned unto fables"(IITim4:3-4).

This is why we see so many new "religions" and new mash-ups and mixtures of beliefs as people try have their own personal religion that is just right for them.

Recently a young man passed along to me a booklet that was a newsletter of sorts with the title of "Science of the Mind". I was told that it contained wisdom for today. I had only intended to skim over it since I was immediately suspicious, but ended up reading it cover to cover. The more I read the more I realized that people are so lost, so blind, and so ignorant of God that they will grab on to anything. The magazine ended up being for this new religion whose founder Ernest Holms has carefully woven many different aspects of various religions into his upper-middle class chic religion. Just from perusing this one magazine I was able to recognize Hindu, Yoga, Buddhism, and Christianity. Many of these hucksters like Holmes, Osteen, and Robbins play to those "itching ears". People are told exactly what they want to hear : "You deserve to be happy." "You deserve to have your best life now." As Ernest Holmes put it, "The God of my understanding assures me that I am worthy of everything I ever wanted and my life is meant to be happy." In another portion of that magazine Ernest Holmes said this: "The Divine (God of my understanding) [notice he gives no credit to the one true God] could only intend good and abundance for its creation, and we need to know that its nature is forever flowing into everything we do." So, does that mean if I cheat on my wife that its nature is flowing? If I beat my kids and my wife, does its nature flow there too? Nowhere in the magazine did it point to any one authoritative book or writings, other than the various writings of the founder himself. A man as the source of so called "true wisdom", really?

Charles Ryrie, a renowned theologian, said, "Theology is for everyone. Theology simply means thinking about God and so expressing those thoughts in some way. In this basic way, everyone is a theologian."[1] If not for the advent of the living word and our Bible, this world would probably not exist as we know it. A real horror story could be written of the distopian society that would dominate completely void of God and and any revelation about Him. I shudder to even think about it.

The Bible is the word of God. Jesus Christ Himself said in a prayer, "thy word is truth"(Jhn 17:17). One of the approximately 40 men directly inspired by God to record His revelation to man, Peter, said, "For the prophecy came not in old time by the will of man: but holy men of God spake as they were moved by the Holy Ghost" (II Pet 1:21). Paul, who wrote over half of our New Testament, gave us the most oft used text about this subject, "All scripture is given by inspiration of God, and is profitable for doctrine, for reproof, for correction, for instruction in righteousness . . ." (II Tim 3:16). The two passages are part of God's word -- Truth. They teach us one important aspect of the doctrine of the Bible -- Inspiration. This is one of what I call "the three I's" which are taught in advanced Theology: Inspiration, Inerrancy, and Infallibility. As I said at the outset, I want to keep this basic so I won't go into those.

Before I discuss the basic structure and layout, etc. of the Bible, I must mention some extra books often associated with the Holy Bible, especially in Catholic ones. These extra books are known as the Apocrypha which means literally "hidden". This term is applied to a collection of books which can number from 13-16 and appear in many Bibles between the Old and New Testaments. The Jewish tradition did not include these books in the Hebrew Canon (from the Gr. Canon - "reed; measure, or standard)[2] of Scripture. Besides the Jews, the early Church fathers nor the Reformers fostered any acceptance either. The Roman Catholic Church, at the council of Trent, went against hundreds of years of accepted norms and included the Apocrypha as part of Old Testament.

When I teach about the Bible I use a simple diagram that I hand out to students. One look at the page shows a clear division with the Old Testament on the left-hand side and under it's title is the text, "39 books written in Hebrew and Aramaic". Under this heading I have the books listed in order running down the left side of the page, but they are grouped together under their respective types of literature. There is The Law with Genesis through Deuteronomy and History with Joshua through Esther, then Poetry with Psalms and Proverbs etc., then Prophecy with all the prophetical books to round out the Old Testament. On the right side of the page is the New Testament with this below it: "27 books written in Greek" and just as with the OT they are in order under headings like Gospels, History, Paul's letters, General letters and Prophecy.

For the many who say they really don't need the Old Testament, I say whoa, wait just a minute. Jesus, whenever he quoted scripture, quoted from the OT! The Old and New Testaments are to be seen together. Jesus was not a Christian. He was a Jew. The OT was the only Bible He had. This is vitally important for one reason which we can find in an early event in the life of Jesus. This event was when Jesus was led into the wilderness to be tempted (just after His baptism). He had been fasting 40 days and was obviously quite hungry. The Devil tried to get Him to turn stones to bread and Jesus answered, "It is written, man shall not live by bread alone, but by every word that proceedeth out of the mouth of God" (Matt 4:4). This was a quote directly from Deuteronomy 8:3 where Israel was crying in the wilderness for bread. During this onslaught by the enemy, our savior used the best defense available to us all -- He told the Devil three times, "it is written". These three words were the perfect way to disarm the Devil. And of course, Jesus knew exactly what was written! The word of God for the Jews at this time was -- guess what? The Old Testament. There is something about the Greek word for our English "it is written" which is gegraptai which means literally "it stands written" and the Greek New Testament grammar conveys an action that is a finished product.

We see this theme often in the word of God -- "Forever, O LORD, thy word is settled in heaven" (Ps 119:89). And, "The grass withereth, the flower fadeth; but the word of God shall stand forever" (Is 40:8). The question invariably seems to pop up especially in this culture of Postmodernism, "Why should we trust the Bible?" It is a well established fact that Jesus Christ was a remarkable man who has made a profound impact upon the world. Given this, it stands to reason that we should investigate what He thought of Scripture. It is quite clear from a careful study of the biblical record that Jesus had the highest esteem for the Old Testament text which was essentially the Bible of the Jews. He recognized that its words were (are) indeed the voice of God.

Although many today consider the stories (and characters in them) which were an integral part of Hebrew culture as just that -- stories, myths and legend, Jesus never questioned such names as Abel, Lot, Elijah, and Job. Some argue that Jesus was just reflecting the views of His time, but for the Christian it goes much deeper than that. He was not just simply a man among the sea of humanity. He was fully man and at the same time He was fully God. He is now glorified. So, it stands to reason that God's own opinion of Scripture is paramount for the Christian.

In the study of theology and/or doctrine the prime focus is the word of God since it's the bible from which that doctrine comes. Though it is obvious that God gave His word by visions, dreams, and prophetic messages that were not all recorded, we also have the Bible. This word of God is a supernatural work which is God's special revelation of Himself and His redeeming purpose through Jesus Christ. To the Christian the Bible is quite credible and infallible. That only makes sense when you consider God is the author. Herein lies the problem with the debate over the Bible. The unconverted -- those not "Born

Again" -- can't fathom such a perfect book, such a supernaturally perfect rule for faith and life. The Southern Baptist Convention's "Baptist Faith and Message" puts it quite well: "The Holy Bible was written by men divinely inspired and is God's revelation of Himself to man. It is a perfect treasure of divine instruction. It has God for its author, salvation for its end, and truth, without mixture of error, for its matter.

Therefore, all scripture is totally true and trustworthy. It reveals the principles by which God judges us, and therefore is, and will remain to the end of the world, the true center of Christian union, and the supreme standard by which all human conduct, creeds, and religious opinions should be tried. All scripture is a testimony to Christ, who is Himself the focus of divine revelation."[3] Jesus once said, " "Heaven and earth shall pass away, but my words shall never pass away" (Luke 21:33)

One of the primary reasons for this work is the pervasiveness of the postmodern mindset that so drives the pulse of today's culture in America and the world. Dr. R. Albert Mohler Jr., President of the Southern Baptist Theological Seminary, said this: "The only way to escape the rationalist claims of modernism or hermeneutical nihilism of postmodernism is the doctrine of revelation -- a return to the doctrine of Sola Scriptura (by scripture-alone)[4]

The battleground for the authority of Scripture is still active, but true Christians are losing ground to Neo-orthodoxy (the new orthodoxy) and liberalism. Both have seeped into the Church and her training grounds -- the {once} distinctly Christian colleges and universities. Dr. Mohler tells of the renowned theologian J.I. Packer who once renounced his involvement in the larger debate over the inerrancy and authority of the Bible. Referring back to 1966 to a conference held at Wenham, Mass. Packer confronted some professors from evangelical institutions who, as they put it officially, "now declined to affirm the full truth of Scripture." That-was-over-50-years-ago!

As I said, the battle is still raging and is by no means over. If man is not to live by bread alone, but by every word from the mouth of God, then Scripture alone is the ultimate authority for life, doctrine, and faith. This is a core Christian doctrine and is really non-negotiable. All who are true Christians in heart and soul must take a stand and give no ground in this!

The winds of false teaching and false doctrine are swirling and gaining strength like the winds of a tropical storm as it becomes a hurricane. It is getting so bad these days, even in the Church, that I believe it may be time for a New Reformation!

Chapter Eight individual study/group disscusion questions;

Do you trust the Word of God 100%? If not, why not?

How do you think Jesus felt about the Word of God?

Is the Bible the words of men to other men or the Word of God to man?

CHAPTER 9

JESUS CHRIST: MESSIAH, SON, LORD

" I believe. . .and in Jesus Christ, His only Son, our Lord . . ." (from The Apostle's Creed)

Most people know basically who Jesus Christ is. As a matter of fact, there are very few who even doubt the historical fact that He is indeed a figure from human history. The great fire in Rome in AD 64 was blamed on "Christians" by Roman historian Tacitus. His record in Latin mentioned one "Christus", a Jew put to death by Governor Pontius Pilate. Yet another Governor, Pliny the younger, wrote to Emperor Trajan around AD 112 complaining about "the spread of these Christians who worshiped one called Christ." There are far too many extra-biblical (meaning outside of the Bible) records to go into it here. Suffice it to say, the Christian claim to the existence of the man called Jesus of Nazareth can hardly be successfully refuted. Many have tried to stop the spread of the fame of the God - man who is savior of the world. As a matter of fact, with the exception of John, all of the Apostles were put to death for preaching about Jesus.

The best source for knowledge about Jesus is found in the New Testament's 27 books. The reason we find within it more than one

Gospel account is simple --eyewitness testimony to the life and teachings of Jesus, the Christ, the Son of God.

What's in a name? We've all heard that old saying. For those in Jewish culture names were very significant and remember Jesus was NOT a Christian He was a Jew! We see the importance of names in God's renaming of Abram to Abraham and Jacob to Israel. I won't go real deep into a name study here, but I will say it is a fascinating and revealing study that every Christian should undertake.

The name Jesus revealed to Mary in Luke 1:31 by the angel Gabriel was very significant for both His identity and His mission. The Hebrew Yehoshua, from which the derivative Yeshua comes, means "God saves" or "God is salvation". We have become accustomed to using the Greek form in calling Him Jesus. What many think is a full name Jesus Christ is not really. Jesus is of course a proper name, but Christ is a title. It comes from the Greek translation of the Hebrew "Messiah" which means "anointed". It was common in Jewish culture to anoint a King, or Priest, or even a prophet. Jesus was no different. It had to be the same for the Messiah to be anointed by the Spirit of the Lord.

Remember the event of the baptism of Jesus when John the Baptist was hesitant to baptize Jesus, but the Lord said, "suffer it to be so now: for thus it becometh us to fulfill all righteousness" (Matt. 3:15). This statement does NOT mean that Jesus came for baptism because He had sinned; He was without sin. This act was an identification with humanity and was a necessary part (as an anointing) of the redemptive process securing the righteousness of Christ for us all. This baptism portrayed for us a foreshadowing of His own death, burial, and resurrection showing us a perfect obedience by the perfect man. Jesus was affirmed by testimony directly from heaven just after this event.

The idea of a "Messiah" or "anointed one" was spoken of in the Torah or Pentateuch which are both names of the first five books of Law in the Old Testament from Genesis to Deuteronomy. Deuteronomy 8:15 says that the LORD will raise up from among the people of Israel a prophet like Moses. The title Christ is synonymous with Messiah. Jesus is the Christ for "God anointed Jesus of Nazareth with the Holy Spirit and with power" (Acts 10:38). He is the one "who is to come" (Luke 7:19), the object of "the hope of Israel" (Acts 28:20).

> Son of God is an oft misunderstood title for Jesus. He used the designation of Himself only rarely, but acknowledged the truth of it when others used it of Him as in Matt 16:16 & 26:63-64. But what does it really mean? Many see it as meaning "offspring of" which is only true in part. It's main meaning is "of the order of".

Remember in the Old Testament that the "sons of the prophets" (I Kings) did not mean literal sons, but "of the order of" the prophets and in Nehemiah we see "sons of the singers" which means "of the order of" the singers. The great theologian Charles

C. Ryrie simplified it this way, "the designation 'Son of God' when used of our Lord means of the order of God and is a strong and clear claim to full Deity." And he goes on to say, "in Jewish usage the term son of (i.e. Bar-Jonah, Bar-Jesus, Ben-Hur, Ben- Ammi) did not generally imply any subordination, but rather equality and identity of nature."[1]

Jesus used the title "Son of Man" (a clear reference to Deity from the book of Daniel) which means The Representative Man. When Christ did use "Son of God" as He did in John 10:36 saying, "...I am the Son of God," many Jews stepped off of Solomon's porch to grab stones to stone Him. Why would they do that? Blasphemy was a stoneable offense, but if He was referring to a simple "offspring" relationship with God as in "sons of God" then He would not have incurred such wrath because at most He was claiming to be an Angel. These Jews knew exactly what He was saying. He was claiming by that title direct equality (Deity) with God!

In John 10:30 Jesus said, "I and the Father are one" -- the Greek neuter form of "one" does not mean they are one person -- but one in perfect unity in their nature and in their actions meaning full equal Deity. The same kind of stoning was threatened when He openly forgave sin. How can anyone who reads the same Bible I read ever say that Jesus never claimed to be God?

Always remember, when faced with such a quandary, that "the natural man (the unregenerate - not born again) receiveth not the things of the Spirit of God: for they are foolishness unto him: neither can he know them, because they are spiritually discerned" (I Cor 2:14). One should not be surprised then, that the Apostles and New Testament writers adorned their testimony and letters with phrases like, "our Great God and Savior, Jesus Christ (Titus 2:13; II Pet 1:1) and "the Lord of Glory" (I Cor 2:8)

Notice that the name Lord is a term which has varied meanings like a ruler or one with great power being called Lord or as a form of address for aristocrats similar to "sir". When used of Jesus the title Lord means a whole lot more than the foregoing. The Greek is KYRIOS, which renders the Hebrew adonai, is what Jews would speak so as not to speak the most sacred covenant name YHWH. This was the name given Moses at the burning bush in Exodus. The resurrection encounter of Jesus with Thomas, who was absent for His first appearance and was quite obstinate saying he would not believe unless he could see and touch Jesus, was very revealing not just for Thomas, but for us as well.

The disciples were gathered; the doors were shut. Thomas was present at this gathering when suddenly, there in the midst of them appeared Jesus. Most of us know the rest; how Jesus had Thomas look at and touch His wounds while admonishing him to stop doubting and to believe. Thomas was overwhelmed and answered, "my Lord and my God" (John 20:28). Right at that moment all doubt fled from Thomas. He was face to face with the risen Lord - his Lord in whom he now fully believed and trusted - the Lord of all.

By taking up the mantle of Apostolic Doctrine and attributing to

Jesus the divine title "Lord", the first Creeds and Confessions of the Christian faith affirm from the earliest times of the organized Church on earth that the power, glory, and honor due God the Father are likewise due to Jesus, The Christ. This is supported when you consider what Paul said to Titus He is our "Great God and Savior". He also said God, "raised Him from the dead and set Him at His own right hand in the heavenly places far above all principality, and power, and might, and dominion and every name that is named, not only in this world, but also that which is to come" (Eph 1:20-21). And "Neither is there salvation in any other: for there is none other name under heaven given among men, whereby we must be saved" (Acts 4:12) -- "That at the name of Jesus every knee should bow . . .and every tongue confess that Jesus Christ is Lord . . ." (Phil 2:10-11).

Herein is the problem of the ages. Its the same as when Jesus asked the disciples, "Whom say the people that I am?" (Lu 9:18) They answered telling Him that some said John the Baptist or Elijah, but Peter, when asked, gave exactly the right answer: "Thou art the Christ, the Son of the Living God" (Matt 16:16).

Here again is that Hebraism "son of" -- Not offspring, but equality of nature. What is so revealing about this is that Jesus told Peter that flesh and blood had not revealed this to him (or the others up to this point) but the Father revealed it to him. Now, the people in general thought him a prophet, much like John the Baptist or Elijah. Herod thought he was John the Baptist come back from the dead as a martyr. Peter saw the beautiful truth that this was God made Man -- Emmanuel -- God with us!

Who do people say that Jesus is today? Again, a prophet along the lines of Mohammad; a Good teacher like Confucius or The Buddha. Those who subscribe that line of thinking, of Him as a mere man from a time in human history, are called unbelievers since they just do not see what Peter and Thomas saw. What is alarming is that those who do see what they saw and recognize Jesus as Christ; as the Son of God; who know the gospel message and do understand the full implications of the atonement, these are believers. That's right, BELIEVERS. Now here's the part where you may need to hold on to these pages and try not to throw this across the room. Not all believers are going to heaven! Not everyone who believes is born again. Belief and Biblical faith are really two very different things. The book of James says, "the devils also believe, and tremble" (Jam 2:19). This is only intellectual assent and that does not cut it! New Testament faith, Gr. Pistueo - does. It means "to have full trust and assurance in". Look, it is just this simple. It is not some deep or lofty theological concept.

Its no secret to those who know me well that I prefer the good 'ole King James Version of the Bible (I do own 8-9 others). In 1611 our English language was far more refined and not so full of slang and idioms. "Believe" in 1611 meant "to hold dear", "to give one's allegiance to", "to give oneself to". Like a commitment of marriage (with it's new identity) it was a highly personal deep and diligent commitment. I like how Chuck Colson put it (remember, we are talking about our Lord and and how we are saved by faith alone), "Just what is 'saving faith'? This is a good question to ask in today's culture, where everything is a subjective choice. 'Making a decision for Christ may be an unhelpfully vague description of what faith entails. Were we REALLY repentant? Did we really intend to cooperate with God in His work and our transformation? God alone knows the heart and whether our Lordship of Christ is genuine." In another place Colson says, "To live as Christians, we must first understand exactly what occurred on the cross when the good thief expressed faith in Christ and was promised eternity. It was an exchange of identities. Christ comes to the cross to die, giving His righteous life for us; we in turn come to the cross to die, surrendering our old sinful life to Him...He then forever lives in us. This is the heart of Christian conversion."[2]

Colson called it an exchange of identities. We come out from under our own lordship where we are firmly ensconced upon the throne of our heart. We literally surrender and submit in true biblical repentance; finally realizing who this Jesus is and what He is for this world -- Savior AND Lord! We can't take Him as Savior if we do not also take Him as Lord! By faith we put our full trust in Him, not ourselves, not our spouse, not our Government/ President, and not our world, but in the one who is Lord of all. The gift of salvation is all about a new life, "Therefore if any man be in Christ, he is a new creature (creation), old things are passed away; behold all things are become new" (II Cor 5:17).

There is quite the theological vocabulary surrounding salvation in Christ Jesus: Repentance, Election, Adoption, Justification, and Regeneration as well as a couple more I may be forgetting. The pure simplicity of the gospel message is all we need!

A dear brother in the Lord, Bobby McGhee, who is an x-con and was once the epitome of a hardened criminal, explained it so perfectly in his awesome testimony (which I was fortunate enough to hear in person): "I was just so tired. Tired of that old life, tired of all the running, tired of that needle in my arm; I was just so tired. I said, 'Lord, I don't understand all this stuff about you, but I believe what your word says about changing a man.

And I'm askin' you now, if you would, please change me – if you'll have me ... please Lord.' I am here and now giving the reader eyewitness testimony to the fact that God answered that man's prayer!

You see, we don't have to understand all doctrine or grasp all of the mysteries or even get ourselves cleaned up before we come to our Lord. Like Bobby did and like I did, we just have to come with all the broken pieces of our life and heart. Bobby and his wife are now in active full time Prison Ministry (for more than a decade) traveling all over the country (as Christsong) visiting prisoners who Bobby calls the incarcerated Church. That, my friends, is how Jesus changes a man, "not just in his brain, but in his heart" says Bobby. This is what being born again or saved is all about.

Saved? Saved from what? Sin and Hell are not very popular subject matter. It all began with The Fall. This is the story of Adam and Eve who disobeyed God and affected all humanity putting us all under a death penalty. God showed them mercy even amidst their curses by promising a Savior. Simply put, "sin is: missing the mark, rebellion, iniquity, wickedness, ungodliness, crime, lawlessness, transgression, and falling away."[3]

When God created us in His image we were to reflect His glory. With the fall that image became marred and caused separation of man and God. "But your iniquities have separated between you and your God, and your sins have hid his face from you, that he will not hear." (Isa 59:2)

Every transgression then is ultimately against God. David understood this quite well as he came before God broken (remember Bathsheba and Uriah) and repentant and said, "Against thee and thee only have I sinned and done this evil in thy sight..." (Ps 51:4a). We also see, "For all have sinned and fall short of the glory of God" (Rom 3:23).

The effects of sin upon the world are obvious -- just look at the top news stories from the past 20 years and it can't be denied. So many feel like religion is something we do to appease our God to rack up more points in the good column than in the bad. So that, if hell does exist, we may just miss it. I don't know about you, but my balance sheet is very lopsided to the bad! There is no "if" when it comes to Hell. It's easy to see why people relegate hell to a place of myth or fabrication -- a non-reality. It's a psychological fact that men suppress the thing they fear most.

In Scripture, Hell is a very real place. It is described as: 1. "everlasting fire prepared for the devil and his angels..." 2. "hell fire where the worm dieth not, and the fire is not quenched..." 3. "The lake which Burneth with fire and brimstone..." 4. "the bottomless pit..." 5. "outer darkness" 6. a place where there will be "wailing and gnashing of he teeth" 7. a place where one cries, "...I am tormented in this flame" and 8. "the smoke of their torment ascendeth up for ever and ever: and they have no rest day or night."[4]

This is why we say saved. Saved from sin and it's curse, it's death penalty, it's effects and Hell. But, saved to what? We have all seen and understand well what sin is and what it has done to man's relationship to God. Most see the reward of the Christian as simply a heavenly home, but it is so very much more. God's perspective of salvation includes His total work in bringing us from condemnation to Justification, which simply means that since no man could ever stand God's righteous judgment and the Law was really never a way to justify but to expose sin, God solved our death penalty situation and hell bound destination by sending His Son to die for our sins and in our place. When we put our faith in Jesus because of this, God imputes (credits our account) the righteousness of Christ (who took all our sin) from us. We are then acquitted or declared righteous. All of this is why God's grace is so amazing. We get to live in total bliss forever with our Lord. If that were all there is to it, that would be enough. To learn more about the "abundant life" promised by Jesus, read God's owner's manual -- The Holy Bible!

Chapter Nine individual study/group disscusion questions;

Have you ever met anyone who did not believe that Jesus of Nazareth existed?

Why did Jesus come to John to be Baptized? We know Jesus had no sin.

What does the title, "Son of man" mean?

Chapter 10

THE SPIRIT OF GOD, THE SPIRIT OF CHRIST, THE HOLY SPIRIT

"...And we believe in the Holy Spirit, the Lord and giver of life, who proceeds from the Father and the Son; who with the Father and the Son together is worshiped and glorified; who spoke by the prophets..."

The Nicene Creed

"But when the Comforter is come, whom I will send unto you from the Father, even the Spirit of Truth, which proceedeth from the Father, He shall testify of Me." (John 15:26)

I consulted a number of books on Theology and Christian Doctrine in preparing this chapter. I was a bit disappointed to find that the Holy Spirit, for the most part, was relegated to other chapters and not given his own place of prominence in the bulk of the material. For the life of me, I can't figure out why this is.

There is no salvation without the Holy Spirit. There is no comfort, no peace, no redemption, and if we get right down to it, no life . Without him there is no Trinity, no Godhead, and no three-in-one God; no Moses, no Samson, no David and no Bible.

It seems to me that the Third Person of the Trinity - the co- equal person known as the Holy Spirit of God – certainly deserves his own chapter, His own special place in any discussion of core Christian doctrine. Thankfully, all our historic creeds gave Him place and prominence, thus affirming this fundamental truth which is anchored in all who believe and profess that which is born of Biblical origin.

The Belgic Confession which came well before the Protestant Reformation, put this doctrine - of the Holy Spirit - into perspective; Article II; The Holy Spirit is true and eternal God- "We believe and confess also that the Holy Spirit from eternity proceeds from the Father and the Son, and therefore is neither made created or begotten, but only proceeds from both; who in order is the third person of the Holy Trinity, of one and the same essence, majesty, and glory with the Father and the Son; therefore, is the true and eternal God, as the Holy Scriptures teach us."

The Holy Spirit is not some power or some indistinct force like in Star Wars ("May the force be with you..."). There are throughout the Bible, personal pronouns like He and Him referring to the Holy Spirit and He was even described as having emotion in Ephesians 4:30 where we learn that we can grieve Him. Not only is He a person like the Father and the Son – He is like them, fully God.

II Corinthians 3:17 Says, "Now the Lord is the Spirit; and where the Spirit of the Lord is, there is liberty." The word 'now' connects this statement to a previous verse referring to Christ. The King James translators correctly rendered the original Greek article to, in essence say, 'not that the Lord is Spirit,' but that 'the Lord is the Holy Spirit' – allow me to extrapolate that out for you; the Lord is God, the Lord is Jesus Christ, the Lord is the Holy Spirit. To make that just a little bit plainer; the Father is God (or Lord), Jesus Christ is God (or Lord) and the Holy Spirit is God (or Lord).

Now I need to say, before we get too deep into this discussion, that the dawn of the Twentieth Century saw a whole new focus and major emphasis develop for The Holy Spirit and His ministry on Earth. The rise and spread of Pentecostalism and Charismatic focus spread through denominations of all types, not to mention the development of dispensationalism's emphasis on works of the Spirit, are the primary driving forces behind this sometimes undue focus. This is not necessarily a bad thing, but much of it has not been spiritually or scripturally guided. The Holy Spirit is not the author of confusion but of peace. Unfortunately, peace is not what we see among many professing Christians today.

Why do we have so many 'sects' or denominations? I believe that if the Lord were to set foot upon the Earth today, He would hang His head, shaking it back and forth in disapproval (just as He is doing from Heaven right now). This, again, is the reason for what you are reading now.

Everyone can't be right, but everyone can be His and still be in unity. We as Christians can disagree a whole lot more graciously than we often do. I'll admit that I, myself, have been guilty. Today, there is an even greater need for careful and solid Biblical teaching on the Holy Spirit. The fact that most people in the church are sorely lacking in decent biblical education, can't be denied. In fact there are many who assume that the Spirit's activity is all just a New Testament phenomenon. Actually, we see He is just as active in the Old Testament. He participated in Creation, Gen 1:2; Job 26:13, He is the very breath of life as in, Gen 2:7 – Other creatures have life because of Him as in Ps 104:29-30.

There are folks from Bible history who would never have been able to do great feats and be victorious in battle without Him (Joshua, Gideon, Sampson). How do you think the word of the Lord came to the prophets? They were moved by the Holy Spirit as in 2Pet 1:21. Ezekiel was even inspired by Him to promise that some day God would put His Spirit in His people in a way that would cause them to live in accordance with His statutes by way of a new spirit and a new heart as in Ez 36:26.

A Christian Manifesto for the Twenty-first Century

I love how Paul put it in his letter to the Ephesians, "In whom (speaking of Christ) ye also trusted, after that ye heard the Word of truth, the gospel of your salvation: in whom also after that you also believed, ye were sealed with that Holy Spirit of promise, which is ernst (guarantee) of our inheritance until the redemption of the purchased possession ..." (Eph 1:13-14). Paul is here talking about the promise in Ezekiel and how it comes to fruition in the one, who by faith and through grace, believes the gospel of Christ and is then given the promise – The Holy Spirit – to dwell within the new Christian as a guarantee or deposit until God's "Purchased Possession" is fully redeemed. Let the reader be aware of the full implication of this passage.

We also saw how Jesus Himself promised the Spirit in His final hours before the cross: "These things I have spoken to you, being yet present with you. But the Comforter (Gr. Paraclete) which is the Holy Ghost (Spirit), Whom the Father will send in my name, He shall tell you all things, and bring all things to your remembrance, whatsoever I have said unto you" (John 14:25-26). That Greek word Paraclete means, "one who is called along side," or "a helper." You will often find names like comforter, counselor, encourager and advocate, etc.

> In the beginning of Acts we see that Jesus kept His promise. The greatest event in the history of the Church, recognized as the birth of the Church was the day of Pentecost. As the 120 were gathered awaiting that promise, "Suddenly there came a sound from Heaven as of a rushing mighty wind, and it filled all the house where they were sitting. And there appeared unto them cloven tongues like as of fire, and it sat upon each of them. And they were filled with the Holy Ghost (Spirit), and began to speak with other tongues (Gr. Glossa-languages) as the Spirit gave them utterance." (Acts 2:2-4).

We see why the Lord told them to go to Jerusalem and wait.

Notice that passage in Acts says they were all filled with the Holy Spirit (Vs 4). Each true believer is baptized into the body of Christ (the church), "For by one Spirit are we all baptized into one body." (I Cor:12:13)

This was a very strategic time in history. The Roman Empire had achieved so much in the way of taming civilization by paving the way for commerce, trade, military, knowledge and forced peace. This is where we get Pax Romana. The famous Peace of Rome that made it possible for Jews to travel from all over the known world and to congregate there in Jerusalem for their main feast day of Pentecost.

As the Holy Spirit had done in the Old Testament in giving men special powers and abilities, he gave these men gathered in that Upper Room whom he now indwelled, the power to communicate in languages unfamiliar to them, but quite familiar to these many foreign Jews. This gift was perfect for this time and place to spread the Gospel of the risen Christ among this sea of people of many nationalities and languages. We see very clearly how the Spirit can empower. He took these pip squeaks huddled together behind closed doors and turned them into powerhouses for God. The crowds were astonished and perplexed. It was obvious that these were unlearned Galileans and fishermen. And yet they could be heard magnifying God in so many languages.

Peter, filled with the Holy Spirit, rose and gave his first powerful sermon, empowered differently by the Holy Spirit and three thousand were added to the church that day!

Okay, this raises a very important question. Most of us understand, at least academically, that the Holy Spirit can empower a child of God, but why do so many live such powerless Christian lives? We must look carefully at the disciples that glorious day. They were assembled and waiting as they were instructed to do. This means they obeyed the words of Christ! So, they were first willing and second obedient and third ready. They were expectant and ready for the promise, even though they could not have known how it would manifest. Some like to give undue focus on the fire and the tongues, but the take away from the Pentecost event is what we saw happen just after the wind, the fire, and the tongues. There is no way that the disciples would have been able, in their own natural abilities, to do what they did in drawing the focus to Christ and his resurrection – no way Peter would have been so bold by proclaiming the Gospel of Jesus the Messiah – the Christ, unless given that power "from on high."

These disciples (and later the apostles) wrought miraculous power – a power not their own, not requested, not called down form heaven, but a power given to willing, ready, and obedient vessels at just the right time, in just the right place so that three thousand souls would call upon the Lord that day! That, my friends, is what the Holy Spirit's work is all about. Not the rushing mighty wind, not the cloven tongues of fire, not the miraculous tongues (languages), but the souls. Three thousand of them which were added to the church that day – three thousand of them crossed over to the best part of eternity that day all because willing and obedient people thought more of their Lord and each other and set aside self so the Holy Spirit could do the rest. None of these new Christians had anything to do with their natural (physical) birth nor did they now in their spiritual rebirth, helped along by Spirit filled believers and Spirit filled preaching focused right where it always is – on Christ; now their Lord and Savior forevermore.

It is my opinion that every true Christian ought to know personally of the supernatural since it is nothing short of supernatural what was wrought in us by the Holy Spirit in precipitating that combination of faith (which is a gift of God) by way of grace in our hearts at that most awesome moment of regeneration. He applied life eternal to our soul. Matthew Henry put it like this: "The Spirit, like fire melts the heart, separated and burns up the dross, and kindles pious and devout affections in the soul, in which, as the fire upon the altar, the spiritual sacrifices are offered up. This is that fire "(the same John the Baptist mentions which Christ came to send upon the Earth" Luke 12:49).

I made a promise to my friend and spiritual father the humble and diligent Tom Farrell that I would share my experience of the supernatural power of God the Holy Spirit.* As I lay broken on the urine stained floor of a county jail, the tears flowing like a torrent for all I had lost, and my only thought playing havoc on my heart and mind was that of wanting to die. I felt a wind, if you will, blanket my whole inner being. I went, in just one moment, from completely broken and utterly hopeless, to calm and absolutely at peace as if a huge weight had been lifted off me. It seemed this weight had always been there ever since I could remember. I felt, down to my very core, the love of the Father, the Son, and the Holy Spirit, but in their oneness (if that even makes sense – I felt the fullness of God) as his love refreshed my soul.

That was not all. For the next couple of hours, I was able to fully understand just how much God loves all men and how much our sins hurt him and our hard hearts grieve him. I could feel how much he wants us all to put away our selfishness and sinful ways to come to him as our Father, to have the Son by faith as Savior and the Holy Spirit as advocate. In this time of revelation to my spirit I lost all worry for the future. I felt washed clean and had full assurance I was secure in the Savior's hands and that he would never leave me.

That experience may not be the same as other folks, but I know what God the Holy Spirit did in me that day. What brought it fully home for me was the realization that I no longer feared death. I knew (like I know my name) that it would be better on the other side because I would be with the Lord! I was also struck by one verse in particular that confirmed what was in my spirit: "and I will pray the Father, and he will give you another comforter (the Holy Spirit) that he may abide with you <u>forever</u>" (John 14:16). That confirmed that my soul could rest easy in this new peace and joy knowing he was with me – no matter what – from now on. No one – not even me – could pluck me from his hand – I am secure in his power, not mine – thank God!

Okay let's recap. The Holy Spirit is a person just like God the Father and Jesus the Son. He is also Deity as are they, eternal and worthy of worship and glory. He has been active from eternity, in creation, in giving life, and coming upon Old Testament men, to indwelling New Testament men. He seals the true believer until the day of redemption. He is called Comforter, Helper, Counselor, Encourager, Paraclete and Advocate. He is the baptism of fire spoken of by Jesus and John the Baptist and this occurs at conversion ("we are all baptized into one body") so, based on true Biblical faith in the risen Lord we are baptized [by-in-with] the Holy Spirit. All believers. All means all and that's all all means.

W. Graham Scroggie once said it like this at Keswick: "On the day of Pentecost, all the believers were, by the Baptism of the Spirit (I Corinthians 12:13), constituted to the Body of Christ and since then every separate believer, every soul accepting Christ in simple faith, has in that moment and by that act been made partaker of the blessings of the Baptism. It is not therefore a blessing which the believer is to seek to receive subsequent to the hour of his conversion"[2]

This is a good time to talk about being, "filled with the Spirit" and what it really means; not what some, though well-meaning, are teaching. The clearest passage of Scripture in the Bible on the subject is Ephesians 5:18 - "and be not drunk with wine, wherein is excess; but be filled with the Spirit." Even as far back as ancient times people understood quite well what it means to be drunk. They knew that alcohol overrides a person's normal behavior and actions making them do things they would never otherwise do when not under an intoxicating influence. We in our day, understand this just as well and the list of substances to cause such behavior has grown quite a bit.

We have already established that all are baptized into one spirit. So why is Paul telling – no commanding us to be filled? The Greek is the imperative which means the act following is our duty and that on a regular, daily basis. Our duty is to be filled with or by the Holy Spirit (not with wine, pot, meth, etc. and not with self). When one takes a closer look at the Pentecost disciple as well as others filled with the Spirit, we find they were completely surrendered, obedient, and above all, humble. They were empowered to do works well beyond their own abilities and skills. (Remember Moses, how he complained to God about his own ability to speak – God set him straight). God has made many quiet, reluctant, and shy men into great leaders and preachers. The reason Paul issued this command is because of people's tendency to "walk in the flesh", to be carnal and worldly and caught up in the affairs of present life. The Greek 'pleoo' for the word 'filled' is packed with meaning. We've already seen how the imperative makes it a duty, but we also see that it is a continuous activity; "keep on being filled." Why?

Doesn't the Holy Spirit baptism take care of that once and for all? No! It does not! The life of the Christian – true believer – is moment by moment and day by day. This is why Luke so accurately recorded the Lord's discipleship mandate thus, "...if any man will come after me, let him deny himself, and take up his cross daily, and follow me"(Luke 9:23). This, like being filled with the Spirit, is a daily self sacrifice and a full reliance upon the Spirit of God to lead one. This is that "life more abundant." When we are willing to be filled or fully influenced by the Holy Spirit, he will penetrate and saturate our whole being with his presence and power.

The question then is not one of having more of Him, but of allowing Him to have more of us!

Chapter Ten individual study/group discusion questions;

Do you approve of all the "denominations" within Christianity?

Did you realize how active the Holy Spirit was in the Old Testament?

Is there a difference between being "Baptized" by the Holy Spirit and "Filled with?"

Chapter 11

"AND I WILL BUILD MY CHURCH"

"And upon this rock I will build my church: and the gates of hell shall not prevail against it..." (Matt. 16:18)

If the whole of the church today could fully grasp the above passage, what a different world we would live in. I mentioned earlier the awesome confession of Peter when the Lord asked, "Who do men say that I am?" (Matt. 16:13). It was obvious that Peter recognized the fullness of God and man in the person of Jesus. His response recorded by Matthew in the Greek definite article "the" ... Son of the living God, was rewarded with the revelation to Peter by the Lord that this faith confession did not originate within themselves or anyone around Him, but from the Father in Heaven: "He saith unto them, but whom say you that I am? And Simon Peter answered and said, Thou art the Christ, the Son of the Living God. And Jesus answered unto him, "Blessed art thou, Simon Bar-Jona-: flesh and blood hath not revealed this to thee, but my father which is in Heaven. And I say also unto thee, that thou art Peter, and upon this rock I will build my church; and the gates of Hell shall not prevail against it." (MT16:15-18)

In the later part of this passage, the Lord used a play on words with

Peter's name, Gr. Petros (Strong's 4704) and rock or Petra (Strong's 4703). The former means stone and the later means rock as in a "Mass of rock" like bedrock. The former as a detached stone, pebble, - a stone easily thrown or moved. The rock is a type of sure foundation[1] and this gives us Christ as our sure foundation. And Peter as the first of new stones added to "build" His church: "...with the saints," and of the household of the God: and are built upon the foundation of the Apostles and the prophets, Jesus Christ Himself being the chief corner stone..." (Paul speaking in Eph 2:20). This is a beautiful picture of NT church. Jesus is the head "Cornerstone," and master builder and the building stones (us) are , as Peter said, "Living Stones" (1st Peter 2:5) added by faith through grace.

The word 'church' in our English Bible is only mentioned twice in the gospels, much more often in the epistles, is from the Greek 'ecclesia' which in its most basic sense means, 'assembly.' It was often used for whenever people gathered for an official function, such as a political oration or proclamation, sporting event, etc. (today we even say "general assembly"). This word 'church' in the theoretical sense is like other terms which contrast from the raw secular meaning. The dictionary definition is: 1) a building for public and especially Christian worship. 2) The whole body of Christians. 3) A denomination. 4) Congregation. 5) Public Divine Worship.[2] Numbers two and five are the closest to being correct for Christians. The church is not an organization, although some say it is, nor is it a denomination, though you often hear "Lutheran Church" or the "Methodist Church"). The church is not a building. It is a "chosen and called out assembly."

Pattering itself after the many local neighborhood Synagogues, the NT church was a local autonomous assembly (congregation) of believers. When Jesus said, "...I will build..." it was recorded dramatically in the future progressive tense and could very well be translated, "...I shall continue to build..."[3] The building began with Peter. The other disciples followed. After Peter's first power packed sermon, three thousand were added to the church that first Pentecost day.

"The statement, "… and the gates of Hell shall not prevail against it" (the church Matt 16:18b KJV) is wrongly understood by many. They think that it means that Hell can't touch us, but that is not what the Lord is saying! Cities and Kingdoms have gates to keep people out. So in this picture hell is not on the offensive -- the church is and the language of, 'shall not prevail' can be understood as 'will not stand against.' The Greek for Hell is Hades which is "the grave" or "death." As Peter stood that day with the rest of the assembly – the church – his sermon blew the gates of Hell right off the hinges, snatching 3000 from ignorance, darkness and death and into marvelous light!

Did you notice that I used the word, kingdom, a moment ago?

One can hardly teach on the doctrine of the church and not mention the Kingdom of God. Sometimes we see it called the Kingdom of Heaven too. There are many who miss the significance of this (I did for years). We see Kingdom of Heaven and/or Kingdom of God much in the Gospels and quite prominently right at the beginning of both the ministry of John the Baptist: "…saying repent ye for the Kingdom of Heaven is at hand…" (Matt 3:2) and of Jesus; "Jesus began to preach, and to say repent for the Kingdom of Heaven is at hand" (Matt 4:17).

When Jesus sent the disciples out two by two, they preached the Kingdom not the Church. However, there is an intimate connection between the Church and the Kingdom of God. Simply put, the Kingdom of God is the rule of God in the hearts of men. The focus of the Kingdom is redemption found only in Christ.

The subjects of the Kingdom are the people of God who accept the full rule of God (accept Christ as lord by grace through faith), so, in essence, Old Testament saints and the church. This does not necessarily mean Israel because, if you remember, Jesus scolding some Jews saying, "You are of your father the devil" (John 8:44).

I'll sum this up by giving five characteristics of the relationship of the church to the Kingdom of God; 1. The Church was given the "keys to the Kingdom." Thereby making her guardian of the way of entry (Mt 16:19). 2. The Church testifies or witnesses to the Kingdom. Jesus said, "The Gospel of the Kingdom will be preached throughout the whole world" (Mt 24:14). 3. The Kingdom builds the Church. Christ is the Head and Focus. He said He would build His Church. People are added by Faith. 4. The Church is not the Kingdom, but a part of it. 5. The Church is the arms and hands of the Kingdom by evangelism and tempering of mercy through love: "...love your enemy...do good unto..."(Luke 6:35). We must not forget that the Kingdom is both present – within us (by the Holy Spirit) and the future of Christ is coming again to rule and reign upon the Earth for 1000 years.

There are a couple of ways to understand the church. There is the universal (called Catholic in the creeds) church of all "true" believers and there is the local church which can be applied to any group of two or more gathered in the name of Christ. There are really large "Worship Centers" holding thousands. In the Bible, Paul wrote to entire cities like Ephesus, or Corinth, "To the church at Corinth..."

An alarming trend must be mentioned at this point to highlight the fact that there are 'true' churches and false, just as there are 'true' believers and false. Whenever a local and/or denominational church sides with the dominant culture/liberal views such as evolution, LBGT issues, abortion or same sex marriage and the like; they are just as guilty and in error as those who peddle false doctrine. Any belief or practice that blatantly contradicts core Christian Doctrine and personal holiness is FALSE. When a group or even an entire denomination stubbornly clings to such ways; they disqualify themselves from Orthodox Christianity and they are just plain wrong. That they adhere to such exposes them as false!

Keep in mind that Orthodox does not mean some strange, foreign, exotic or radical way of thinking. It means; "adhering to a traditional and established doctrine – commonly accepted, customary."[4] I am often accused of being all doom and gloom when I warn of such trends as the foregoing but somebody has to awaken people to alarming trends such as secular humanism, post modernism and liberal theology. Francis Schaeffer once said that, "Liberal theology is only humanism in theological terms."[5]

One of the distinctive features of the future role of the Anti- Christ is not just one world government and one world monetary system but one world religion. I can see the beginning threads of this in what many call "Christian" in today's culture, but is really the future church of the tribulation's Antichrist.

The "true" church must have a purpose. Remember the keys given to Peter and the church? We who make up the church have the keys to the Kingdom in our gifts of preaching and teaching, serving and showing mercy. We may very well be, all the 'Bible' people will ever experience. The glory of God in Christ is the ultimate goal: "Unto Him be glory in the church by Christ Jesus..." (Eph 3:21 KJV). And in that same letter Paul wrote, "And He gave some apostles; and some prophets; and some, evangelists; and some pastors and teachers; for the perfecting of the saints, for the work of the ministry, for the edifying of the body of Christ." (Eph. 4:11-12)

The church does not have one singular purpose and the diversity of purpose of the church can be thought of as ministry. Ministry to God through corporate worship, to fellow believers and, of course, to the world via evangelism. Some have lost focus by not striking a healthy balance in ministry. There are huge segments of the Christian community who place undue focus on worship as if that is all there is to the whole of the Christian experience. The evidence speaks for itself in the financial statements of huge global ministries whose spending on music, lighting, venue and production etc. far outstretches spending on edification and education of the church body in proper doctrine and Bible by over six times.[6] This is a very sad statistic and one that ought not to be. Worship certainly has its place and to be fair, there are also segments of the church which place very little focus on this very important aspect of ministry. Paul taught the Collossian church, Let the word of Christ dwell in you richly in all wisdom; teaching and admonishing one another in psalms and hymns and spiritual songs, singing with grace in your hearts to the Lord. (Col 3:16) Here is this from a great Bible Dictionary; "The very concept of worship is often {properly} defined as ascribing worth and honor to the Triune God... and is in a broader and encompassing sense, to be understood as an interrelation between divine action and human response."[7] The main root word in the Greek is proskuneo and pictures prostrating oneself. Our English word comes from 'worthship'. Jesus made a very classic statement when He told the Samaritan woman and poked some pretty big holes in her ideas as to worship by saying, "God is a spirit and they who worship Him must worship Him in spirit and in truth" (John 4:24). Tradition, ceremony and ritual are never the heart of the matter, but sincerity of heart – an attitude and not an outward form – a lifestyle of prostrated submission is.

Yet another purpose of the church is that of edification or
building up of the Body of Christ. The clearest scripture on this is in Ephesians chapter four where Paul is teaching about spiritual gifts; " For the perfecting of the saints, for the work of ministry, for the edifying of the body of Christ: til we all come into the unity of the Faith, and the knowledge of the Son of God, unto a perfect man, unto the measure of the stature of the fullness of Christ" (Eph 4:12-13). "Perfecting" here does not mean mere perfecting of morality, but has the same connotation as that of getting a soldier ready for his commanding officer. This process of sanctification makes one fit for the master's use but also fit to edify the bretheran; "'til we all come into unity of the faith" – that body of truth that is the Gospel. The Gospel is salvation in Christ and other truths is doctrine of the Apostles. "Once delivered to the saints" (Jude 3).

I am dumbfounded how anyone can read that Ephesians passage and think it is alright to imagine our only goal is to bring souls to Christ and then leave them to their own devices! Paul, again, said it so beautifully to the Colossian church, "Christ in you the hope of glory: whom we preach, warning every man, and teaching every man in all wisdom; that {WE} may present every man perfect (as a mature believer) in Christ Jesus" (Col 1:27b-28).

Bringing souls to Christ should be the heart and soul of the Evangelicals duty in Christ! This is not something we leave only to a select few in "missions." The popular terminology for this these days is "missional movement". The great commission (Mt 28:18-20) is the responsibility of every church member and is not merely to serve just in our own church, but those in one's own sphere of influence in and outside the church, at the corner market, at the mall, in one's neighborhood, city or town. Jesus gave us the perfect example of looking out for other's needs all around us and making them our mission by sharing the Gospel in word and deed. We are to comfort the sad, visit the sick and the prisoner, take care of widows and orphans, help the poor, and show mercy and reconciliation to one another. This is not just to be done in our community but everywhere we go.

Remember those 3000 souls? "Then they that gladly received his word (Peter's) were Baptized – and the same day there were added unto them (the newly formed church) about three thousand souls." (Acts 2:41)

Baptism and the Lord's Supper, what most Protestants call 'ordinances', are important aspects of the church. Some call these two, 'Sacraments.' The word sacrament, like holy, means sacred and set apart, dedicated to God. We see in some translations the word mystery or Latin, musterion. This explains its use among Catholics and Lutherans who place a focus on the mystery of the elements (bread and wine) and Transubstantiation (the belief that the elements of bread and wine are actually changed into the body and blood of our Lord) and for Lutherans, consubstantiation (the belief that, while the elements remain the same, the actual presence of the Lord is in, under and throughout them). The groups that prefer sacrament over ordinance also say they are a "means of grace" meaning they convey grace to the recipient.

Most of the Protestant denominations use the word 'ordinance' as a sort of synonym for 'sacrament' but without the idea of a works based acquisition of grace. Focus is thereby given its proper place in the symbolism. Most Protestants observe only two ordinances while Catholics and Lutherans observe many more. They call them Sacraments.

Baptism over the centuries has been, unfortunately, very controversial. Mode, i.e. immersion, dipping, or sprinkling;

implications (does it save?); in what name? Just Jesus or Father, Son and Holy Spirit? And finally, who do we baptize? (Infants, children or just adult believers?) Overwhelming evidence from scripture itself along with much writings from the early church Fathers, support immersion and its symbology of the new believers identification with the death, burial and resurrection of Christ. We go down into the water = death; we are in/under water = burial; we come up out of the water = resurrection. Baptism in Greek means "to dip, to immerse, to submerge, and or even to plunge" The word has it's roots in the ancient Jewish rite of purification; (the old man dies and the new man emerges), initiation and identification (with the people of God). John the Baptist made his mission clear. His baptism was one of repentance.

Baptism is normally sought as soon as is practical as it is seen as the beginning of the Christian Life. It would not be fair of me if I were not very clear on the fact that Baptism is not part of Salvation. It is as Peter said,"The answer of a good conscience toward God..." (1st Peter 3:21). This ordinance is our public declaration of faith (an outward show) of an inward change. We declare that we have joined with Christ by faith, then identify with Him in Baptism.

Many who advocate "baptismal regeneration," (that baptism actually causes regeneration) use Acts 2:38 as their proof text; "Then Peter said unto them, 'Repent and be baptized every one of you in the name of Jesus Christ {for} the remission of sins, and ye shall receive the gift of the Holy Ghost.'" Notice that the people had asked what they should do and Peter gave the exact formula for their ills. 1. Repent. That is step one. He did not say to get baptized first. Repentance means a change of mind, will, and direction, away from sin and sinful ways – and toward Jesus Christ (God) whose sacrifice on the cross made it possible to have sins remitted.

Our little English word, 'for' is actually the Greek word, 'eis' which means "as a result of" or "on the basis of." Lets try that plugged into Acts 2:38 to see if it changes how we understand the passage: "Repent everyone of you and be Baptized {as a result of} the remission of sin..." or "Repent everyone of you and be Baptized {on the basis of} the remission of sin.

The key to understanding this properly is Repentance and Faith. This is why Peter said 'repent' first because repentance is inextricably linked to faith which when exercised (because of grace) remits sins, paving the way to regeneration long before any water is applied. We don't have to fully understand all the inner workings of the supernatural grace of God. All we need to know is that He gave His only begotten son as the once and for all sacrifice for our sins. All we have to do is take the first step – repent. (Remember, only Godly sorrow works repentance as in 2Cor 7:10). The second step was then Baptism, the outward expression as well as public declaration of an inward change. Unless we repent based on Faith, baptism is useless to us.

The wealth of evidence in the NT as to who is baptized seems to support those who were under preaching or they "who received his word" (Peter) or who were instructed as was the eunuch under Philip, those of Samaria as well who were under his preaching, were baptized ..."when they believed... both men and women." (Acts 8:12). There does not seem to be clear NT precedence for infant baptism. Then there is the matter of what name? (Just Jesus Christ or Father, Son and Holy Spirit?) Who is authorized to baptize etc.? Scripture is our guide and if a particular method or minor doctrine goes contrary to Holy Writ then I say it is invalid.

Let me make this really simple; If I find a true NT Bible believing, Bible preaching church that exemplifies balance in worship, fellowship, teaching/preaching and evangelism, then I don't care if they dunk me (three times or just one), or if they baptize in the name of Jesus Christ only or in the Trinity. I don't care if the pastor does the baptizing or if my best friend in the church does it. I don't care if it is done down in the river or in the church's beautiful Baptistery Font as long as the Community of believers is there to rejoice with me.

There have been so many divisions caused by very insignificant details of Baptism and many many other things in the Church. The

Church, the people of God, should be embarrassed. Identity with the church universal is about unity: "Now I beseech you, brethren, by the name of our Lord Jesus Christ, that ye all speak the same thing, and that there be no divisions among you; but that ye be perfectly joined together in the same mind and in the same judgment." (1Cor 1:10)

So if one church sprinkles or if another church baptizes infants – "Who art thou that judgest another man's servant? To his own master he standeth or falleth. Yea, he shall be holden up: for God is able to make him stand," (Rm 14:4) I am not going to forego fellowship or fail to consider my church family because of very minor 'rib issues' as a friend of mine once said.

The Lord's Supper is the second ordinance of the church. It is also called communion. To me, this ordinance is one of the most important among our practices as Christians. We use the elements of bread and wine (or just juice which is still fruit of the vine) to represent symbolically the body and blood of our Lord. I believe it is vitally important to understand fully that Jesus taught His disciples on the last Passover that He would share with them in a human form.

Far too many overstep the scriptures in some pretty elaborate ideas like Transubstantiation and Consubstantiation. I'm sure whoever came up with these ideas were well meaning, but there is just no clear support for such in scripture. To understand the symbolic nature of this memorial one must see it for what it is – just that, a memorial.

Many times scholars think they have God figured out in regard to this doctrine or that theological concept only to find out later that they probably overthought an idea or misspoke a particular notion causing more harm than good. When we look closely at the Lord's Supper, we need to identify what was actually going on…Passover! These disciples at the table, as yet, were not enlightened as to deep spiritual truth (remember, Pentecost was yet future).

Very simply, what the Lord did on this Passover celebration was to take one long time Symbolic Memorial and institute a new one. This new one had a very different sacrifice – His own body and blood. To make of such a solemn memorial more than what scripture bears out is, in my humble opinion, irresponsible. Our Savior Himself outlined and modeled this communion without technical jargon or deep theological hoops to jump through. These were simple uneducated men in His company. Up to this very night many ideas and parables had gone right over their heads, but this night was a bit different.

Jews had been celebrating Passover for nearly 1500 years.

There was no mystery or over-spiritualization of this very simple memorial. The lamb was the central element. Its blood was another (it was placed on the doorposts and lintels) and the death of the first born was an obvious supernatural act of God. It brought Egypt to its knees in its impact and wide spread nature. Thus allowing God's will – their deliverance out of captivity in a hostile country. When Moses taught the Israelites about Passover, he said it would be observed year after year as a lasting ordinance to remind God's people of where they had been.

Now Christ acts all of it out as He re-institutes a new ordinance (similar to the old). This new ordinance is different because Jesus Himself is the lamb. The head of the house during Passover would lift the platter of unleavened bread high above the table and announce, "This is the bread of affliction" – now the Lord lifts bread and says, "This is my body..." and later the cup was lifted and he announced, "This cup is the new testament in my blood...". That was the seal of redemption – His blood being shed for us to ensure our being passed over by the second death. After proclaiming the blood of the New Testament – the new covenant, He said, "As oft as ye drink it, in remembrance of me. For as oft as ye eat this bread and drink this cup, ye do show the Lord's death til He come." (1Cor. 11:25-26) Sounds awful simple doesn't it? It is just that simple. There is no mysterious supernatural change in the elements or grace being conveyed – it is simply a memorial just like Passover. That in no way lessens its importance, but should help to keep us focused on the right idea behind our Lord's sacrifice and His soon return.

This ordinance when practiced by the very early church was intimately connected to Fellowship, hence our calling it 'Communion'.

The fellowship of believers assembled together to share in the Lord's Supper in union, recognizing His very presence as they memorialize His death, but are assured of His second coming.

The best records of the early church fathers seem to be for baptized believers. I, personally believe in open communion, which is that all baptized believers present may partake, not just members of a particular congregation. Just as in Baptism, there are facets of this ordinance which tend to cause divisions, but we must all remember that we believers are to give (double) honor to those over us – our Pastors and Elders. We may not always agree, but that does not excuse us from scriptural submission to God's chosen leaders and to each other. Don't get me wrong here – I'm not saying to go along to get along, but God's chosen elders are chosen by Him (and us) because of God's gifting and wisdom. If we focus less on self and more on each other and on our roles in the body, then we will certainly look and act like a true New Testament Church.

Chapter Eleven individual study/group discussion questions;

What has always been your definition of "Church"?

Did it surprise you or make you think when you learned the truth about the passage, Matt 16:18?

Were you surprised at the meaning of, "Kingdom of God"? Why?

Have the ordinances been a source of confusion for you? How did you settle it?

Chapter 12

CONCLUSION

"Can the liberties of a nation be thought secure when we have removed their only firm basis, a conviction in the minds of the people that these liberties are the gift of God? That they are not to be violated but with His wrath? Indeed, I tremble for my country when I reflect that God is just; that His justice can not sleep forever." Thomas Jefferson

I tremble for my country too, when I see horrors of the day stacking up in unprecedented numbers. Early on I had asked, "Has the world gone mad?" The world – yes, but even more so, our country! As I began to work on this concluding chapter the month of August, 2019 was at a close and in just that past 31 days there had been, that I know of, six mass shootings with nearly sixty dead. First in Virginia Beach, Virginia at the Municipal Center, a public utilities employee shot twelve people in a rampage. the second was at the Garlic Festival in Gilroy, California (four dead). The third was at a Wal Mart in El Paso, Texas (twenty-two dead) and the forth was outside a bar in Dayton Ohio (ten dead). Fifth was a very rural county in Virginia which sees few murders, but one crazed 19 year old man killed his mother, sister and two year old nephew (three) dead at the hands of someone who was called, "Just a normal kid." And last was a disgruntled oil worker who shot to death seven people at random, while wounding twenty-five more.

This is indeed the time and place, at least in American history, to make that clarion call. Why is society in such a mess? That's easier to answer than people want to admit. We have allowed the Serpent (the Devil) to take up residence in our Eden – to whisper in our young people's ears that they are just another creature among the animals – they are a random blip in the cosmos of nothing which came from nothing and leads to nothing, all by pure chance.

This began to unfold within Eden's school houses. Then the Serpent slithered, unabated, into our entertainment. 88% of the public agree that our TV, movies, music etc. is not at all what it used to be. It is not at all clean and wholesome as it once was. The Serpent has rounded out a three pronged attack plan by influencing , and now dominating, our media, print, internet, and broadcast selling America on ideas like abortion as "women's reproductive health" and same sex marriage as an unalienable right among so many other moral lapses.

Technology and Science have indeed done many great things, but they have failed in the quest to solve man's greatest ills. One glance through a newspaper or just 30 minutes of broadcast news will confirm this! I hate to be the bearer of bad news, but none of it is slated to get any better: And then shall many be offended, and shall betray one another, and shall hate one another. And many false prophets shall rise, and shall deceive many. And because iniquity shall abound, the love of many shall wax cold. (Mt 24:10-12 Paul weighed in on this as well and told us exactly what was going to happen (is happening now): "This know also, that in the last days perilous times shall come. For men shall be lovers of their own selves, covetous, boasters, proud, blasphemers, disobedient to parents, unthankful, unholy, without natural affection, trucebreakers, false accusers, incontinent, fierce, despisers of those that are good, traitors, heady, highminded, lovers of pleasures more than lovers of God;" (2Tim 3:1-4)

In the foregoing, Paul was telling Timothy what it would be like in the last days. The same with the earlier passage where Jesus was warning the disciples of the days before the end.

WAKE UP WORLD!! Very large portions of the Bible foretell future events. Much of Bible prophecy has already come true exactly as it was foretold! Any Christian who has done due diligence and read the Bible through more than just casually, knows this is true. No other ancient writings ever in the history of the world ever produced literally hundreds and hundreds of prophecies, many of which have been fulfilled exactly to the letter as they were written centuries before. The point is, we know, from God Himself, how it's all going to end.

God's word is not an open book to everyone. If you'll remember how clueless the disciples were as Jesus taught. Remember also what powerhouses they were after Pentecost? God wants His people to know and trust that He is sovereign and in control of all this world and universe. Bible prophets were the reformers of their day calling Israel back to pure worship and obedience to God. Who speaks for God in our day? The charlatan televangelists? I sure hope not! No, it should be the pastors, preachers, evangelists, and teachers. But, are they on message?

By and large – NO!

If you were about to step off a curb into the path of an oncoming bus, would you want those on the curb to remain silent and just watch you meet your end? Of course not! But many on that curb don't even recognize a bus! Others should shout out to get your attention, right? Are we, who claim to be children of the living God, warning our neighbors to watch out for the steep cliff that leads straight to hell? Sure, they are going to knee-jerk complain that we are judging them, but that is what we all have done and do when we are dead wrong. Deep down they know it. Of the professing, church-going Christians, we see that the pews are far too warm from the backsides of "so-called" evangelicals who really think evangelism is the job of only deacons and "clergy"!

Let's recap what we've covered (with a tad extra) so far. It certainly does look like the world has gone mad! With the opioid crisis, weekly mass shootings, gender fluidity (Facebook's over 70 choices for one's gender), and let's not forget the same old war over abortion with multitudes still arguing about women's reproductive rights over against common sense morality. We have seen a massive assault on the truth by Post-Modernism and Secular humanism's relativistic mindset which seeks to remove any and all Godly standard in order to circumvent personal responsibility to that standard.

Thankfully, we have a select few who recognize truth and defend it. John MacArthur said, "the ultimate truth is an objective reality. Truth is truth whether we accept it or not. The fact that we don't believe a certain thing does not render it untrue." [1]

This country recently expressed its' disgust with the political climate by electing Donald Trump as their president. Democrat – Republican, Liberal – Conservative – these terms are not the same as they once were, even just a century ago. It has all become, as Trump put it, "a cesspool". The country is in an obvious sharp decline in moral standards and once decent traditional values. This decline and decay has been at the hands of extreme left secularists and socialists foisting God out and creating buzzwords like "diversity", "acceptance", "inclusion" and catchy slogans like "Black Lives Matter" (but you can still kill babies).

Science has suffered the same fate having gone off the rails regarding God's six days of creation which has been replaced by a "theory" with little to no evidence. Even the old "Global Warming" crowd changed its banner to "Climate Change". They have even eased up on the oft public declaration of it all being "man-made" now placing the blame quietly on fossil fuels. Why have they done this? In the face of pure science, they are beginning to see that man's impact on global climate is about as serious as a fart in a hurricane. How do you think the ice sheet that once covered nearly half of North America receded?...Oh, yeah, climate change. And that was before the first car ever showed up! Take the time to study both sides diligently and you will see for yourself.

We learned how the very early church developed creeds to affirm

Biblical Apostolic doctrine. A creed encompasses our unchanging Christian doctrine which Jude urged believers to contend for: (Jude 1:3 KJV) "...to write unto you and exhort you that ye should earnestly contend for the faith which was <u>once</u> delivered unto you," [emphasis mine]. "Once delivered" means it is settled – set right there in the Scripture.

In the remaining chapters we covered what is known as Orthodox Christianity. We can thank the courageous Reformers from the 12th through the 16th centuries for paving the way by their sacrifices to contend for the faith even to the point of death. The word Orthodox refers to the essentials that all <u>true</u> Christians have always believed. The great C.S. Lewis called it "Mere Christianity".

It is my deeply-held conviction that a creed or The Creed is by no means obsolete and is needed more so in this day and age of truth by slide rule. The Church has been shaken badly by the enemy. Her foundations are battered and compromised across the globe. Pure theology and doctrine have been hi-jacked and rewritten so many times that many do not know what to believe or even why they believe what they do!

When the challenge to approach this manifesto presented itself, I was elated and pensive at the same time. To think I could be privileged to stand on the shoulders of the great Francis Schaeffer and echo that clarion call to all Christians. We need to put aside petty differences and "get real" as the kids say. It's the 21st century! Do you really think God's patient mercy will hold out for another 75-100 years or more? I don't!

I had first thought to write a newly revised creed, but then I thought better of it. The Nicene Creed, found in the previous chapter on Creeds, Confessions, and Catechisms is more than perfect. Our Christian forefathers laid down this foundational creed based fully on the word of God, and it has stood now for nearly 1700 years. I am sure there are some who would disagree, but I believe we should all be reciting this Creed (as the Catholics do) regularly. It certainly couldn't hurt and may even help keep us all on the same page doctrinally.

By and large there are two main opposing world views out there in the world today: the Secular Humanist and the (God- centered) Christian one. The two have struggled for dominance for at least the last two millennia. Yes, we have always had wars, violence, crime, and decay, but we have also seen distinctly Christian foundations to under gird society, keeping out and out evil at bay.

Take a moment and imagine culture as a fast-moving river with multiple sources. As to the Christian influence which once dominated, we now see only three "Christian" streams that feed the flow: 1) Culture Christians, 2) Congregation Christians, and

3) Christians of Conviction. Now take away the unbelievers first, then numbers 1 and 2 and what is left, unfortunately, is a small trickle in danger of disappearing in drought. What once was a healthy flow of living waters is now barely even a decent stream.

A close associate of Billy Graham, Ed Stetzer gave some blistering insight into this trend, "As a result of the collapse of mainline Protestantism and the growth of secularism, convictional Christianity has incrementally moved outside the American cultural stream. - You see the lanes moving apart, and people who are moving in a more secular direction are now part of the mainstream."[2]

Things have gotten so bad that a recent Lifeway Research Poll revealed 79% agree (somewhat or strongly) that "Christianity today is more about organized religion than loving God and loving people." And in another polling: 44% agree (somewhat or strongly) with "Christians get on my nerves."[3]

I'm just going to lay it out there for you. The enemy is no longer at the gates. He has been allowed to slither right into our midst, and the sad thing about that is…we let him in! Where were our watchmen? The enemy is no dummy. He knows that the best way to destroy a family, neighborhood, community or church is right from within by a calm, patient, slow-working poison called secular-humanism in all its forms.

Matthew Kelly, a Christian and a corporate consulting/ business guru, as well as avid author, said this; "The current secular culture is bankrupt – and becoming more so with each passing day. Today's culture is becoming harsher, colder, increasingly brutal and plagued with an attitude of every man and woman for themselves. People are starting to see this and they are fed up."[4] But here is the sad fact that goes right along with that: they are simply fed up with Christians. Why? Simple. Modern Christians, for the most part, blend right in with the culture. Don't believe me? Watch the Hillsong channel for just 30 minutes and you will see. Now don't get me wrong, there are genuine believers in their ranks – but my bet is, not very many. Remember the false believers I told you about earlier? These are the ones who haven't gotten it. They are still wearing their crown and sit firmly upon the throne of their heart. They are victims of what John MacArthur calls, "easy believism' which is a false gospel that has produced folks no different from the society in which they live. "But they believe," someone will argue. Well, guess what? The devil and his demons also believe, but the book of James says they tremble at the name of Jesus (James 2:16b KJV). They will share the fate of these folk: "Not everyone who says to me 'Lord, lord' will enter the Kingdom of Heaven, … I will tell them plainly, "I never knew you, away from me you evil doers!" (Matt 7:21 & 23).

Does the term 'Hypocrite' sound familiar? That is how society sees most of the Christian community today. I know that some of it is to be expected and comes with the territory, but it is far more prevalent than it should be. Okay, how do we solve this dilemma? We who are true Christians need to unite and spark a new reformation. We need to learn what it is to be genuine Christians. We must first realize that it is not about us. God put humans on this earth for two very simple reasons. These two reasons are what all of existence boils down to; 1) To love God (and to worship Him) supremely with all of our heart, mind, soul and strength and 2) To love our neighbor as we love ourselves. It really is that simple. We are here, <u>not for self</u> <u>!</u> This makes it clear that our life, which we have been so diligently trying to carve out in this world, is not really ours! God gives us our very breadth and numbers our days as in Isa. 42:5 and Job 14:5. We are born to serve.

This is why I have written this book. To clarify who and what a Christian is and the faith we hold – what we believe and why. When I see polls like the one that just came out of the U.K. Which revealed that fewer than half of U.K. Christians, 46%, do not believe Jesus died and rose again for the forgiveness of sin. What? Then how are they Christians? This poll proves they are not!

Our only source of truth is Jesus Christ who is not just revealed in the Bible but also in the hearts of the truly born again. Now is the time to make a priority of being authentic Christians (little Christs) and discipling others to that same end as we have been commissioned by our Lord. This is how we become that "salt" and "light" He said we should be.

We can't keep sitting on the sidelines, saying that "I know we need to change" or "I know I'm not living right." Okay then, Stop it! If you know as I do, that this world is in deep trouble, then it is time. Time for a new reformation, first on a personal level. Then we take that fire we've kindled and go forth to help it spread.

When I was a teen, I met up with some friends at a campsite. I was late and the last to arrive. The fire they had going was so small and pitiful. There was this handful of twigs and leaves that were not going to keep us warm or produce enough light. I proceeded to gather up plenty of thick brush and nice sized kindling and logs to keep us warm and well lit.

This is how the Christian life should be. We've been redeemed and we need that light and warmth and share it with others who will band with us in Christian unity to share the gospel of Christ with the world (or our little part of it.) The secular culture wants to throw a bucket of water on our faith and put out the passion we have for the souls around us. If all we have are twigs and leaves to begin with, they will succeed.

Jesus said, "...in the world ye shall have tribulation: but be of good cheer; I have overcome the world" (John 16:33b). When we accept Christ by faith, we too can overcome the world or at least our tendency to go with the flow of the culture around us. Maybe we can't affect the whole world, but we can make a difference in our little corner of it. So, right now take a stand and make a commitment to be an authentic Christian – a Christ follower – and ask the Lord to light a fire of Reformation (and repentance) in your soul. If you like, use this prayer;

> My Lord and my God,
>
> I now humble myself before you.
>
> I know I have not been all You have wanted me to be and I am, in my heart of hearts, sorry.
>
> I confess that I have sinned against you and ask you to now light a fire of reformation in my soul and heart. I bring you all of me; not just my 'want to,' but 100% of my heart – the good, the bad and the ugly. Please renew me and make me into the person you created me to be – not my will, but thy will, Lord.
>
> Show me the way and I will walk therein.
>
> In Jesus' name, Amen.

A Christian is a disciple. A disciple is a disciplined learner and follower of Jesus who conditioned that relationship thus; "If any man will come after me, let him deny himself, and take up his cross daily, and follow me." (Luke 9:23) But keep in mind that Jesus also said, "For whosoever will save his life shall lose it: but whosoever will lose his life for my sake, the same shall save it." (Luke 9:24) That is the challenge. Self-denial and self-sacrifice! Self or Christ? For the Christian, sure of the faith, the choice is quite clear. I had to learn the hard way, but surrender is oh so sweet! Jesus is the way, the truth and the life, thanks be to God through Him. Amen

Chapter Twelve individual study/group discussion questions;

Who speaks for God today?

Do you think most Americans (or the world), believe most of what they hear in the News or in the classroom?

Who is responsible in Society to keep the evils at bay? Explain your answer.

FOOTNOTES

Introduction: {1} Dictionary of Theological Terms ©2013 Alan Cairns rep by Mt. Zion Church (Chapel Library), Pensacola, FL
{2} How Now Shall We Live -- Chuck Colson & Nancy Percy ©1999 Tyndale Carol Stream, IL

Chapter 1: {1} 2018 World Almanac And Book Of Facts - ©2018 Info-base
{2} The Audacity Of Hope - Barack Obama ©2006 Crown Publishers, New York - p218
{3} ibid #1
{4} ibid #1
{5} Dave Barton- Foundations Of Freedom DVD Series ©2008 Wallbuilders
{6} "People In Pain" Jamie Dean ,June 30, 2018 World Magazine
{7} "Amorite America" 1pg tract PMI Center For Biblical Studies - Dr. Mike Johnston
{8} "Understanding The Times" excerpt ©2012 by Chapel Library, Mt. Zion Bible Church, Pensacola, FL from 2009 Creation College Address by Ken Ham
{9} ©2010 Wallbuilders

Chapter 2: {1} "The Truth War" - John MacArthur ©2007 Thomas Nelson pXX
{2} American Heritage Dictionary, Fifth Ed. ©2012 Dell Mass Mkt Ed.
{3} "Philosophy Made Simple" 2nd Ed., Richard H. Popkin, PhD. ©1993, Doubleday, New York
{4} "The Philosophy Book" DK Publishing ©2011 U>S> and London, Gandeau, Szvdek, Tomley

Chapter 3: {1}The Columbia Encyclopedia ©1976 Columbia Univ. Press
{2} 2018 World Almanac And Book Of Facts ©2018 Info base

Chapter 4: {1} American Heritage Dictionary, Fifth Ed. ©2012 Dell Mass MKT Ed.

{2} Merriam Webster Collegiate Dictionary ©2006 Merriam Webster
{3} Dictionary of Theological Terms ©2013 Alan Cairns rep by Mt. Zion Church (Chapel Library), Pensacola, FL
{4} "Culture Warrior " ©2006 by Bill O'Reilly, Broadway Books
{5} "Conservative Comebacks To Liberal Lies" Gregg Jackson ©2007 JAJ Pub.
{6} "Dissecting Liberal Media Bias" Human Events 10-4-2004 p24
{7} "The Recent Fake News Flurry" Nicholas Thompson & Fred Voglestein ©2018
{8} "If Enemies Haven't Showed Up In Your Life, It's Because You Haven't Showed Up In Theirs" Janie B. Cheney, World Magazine 11-24-2018

Chapter 5: {1} Merriam Webster Collegiate Dictionary ©2006 Merriam Webster
{2} Ibid.
{3}The Old Scofield Reference Bible, Oxford Univ Press, 1917, 2013
{4} Systematic Theology, Wayne Grudem ©1994, Zodervan

Chapter 6: {1} "A Christian Manifesto" Francis A. Schaeffer (Revised) 1982, Crossway p20
{2} Zondervan Handbook to the History of Christianity, Jonathan Hill, ©2006 Zondervan

Chapter 7: {1} "Systematic Theology", Wayne Grudem ©1994, Zodervan p141
{2} American Heritage Dictionary, Fifth Ed. ©2012 Dell Mass MKT Ed.
{3} "Philosophical Foundations For A Christian Worldview" Moreland & Craig ©2013, IVP
{4} "The Question Of God" Armand Nichol, ©2002 Simon & Schuster / Free Press p6
{5} "Fundamentals Of The Faith" John MacArthur, ©1991-2012

Chapter 8: {1} "Basic Theology" Charles C. Ryrie, ©1986, SP Pub. Inc. p9
{2} Systematic Theology", Wayne Grudem ©1994, Zodervan (glossary)
{3} "The Southern Baptist Faith And Message" ©2000 SBC
{4} "Why We Protest" R. Albert Mohler, Tabletalk Mag., Oct. 2017

Chapter 9: {1} "Basic Theology" Charles C. Ryrie, ©1986, SP Pub. Inc. p9
{2} "The Faith" (Participants Guide), Chuck Colson & Gary Poole,©2008 Zondervan p43-44
{3} Basic Theology" Charles C. Ryrie, ©1986, SP Pub. Inc. p212
{4} 1. Matt. 25:41
2. Mk. 9:47-48
3. Rev. 21:8
4. Rev 9:1-2
5. Matt. 8:12
6. Matt. 13:42
7. Lu. 16:24
8. Rev 14:11

Chapter 10: {1} Matthew Henry's Commentary on the whole Bible, © 1991 – 2001 Hendrickson Publishers, Inc. P. 2067
{2} Quote from "The Holy Spirit" - Billy Graham, © 1978 Billy Graham Evangelical Assn., Warner Books Ed.

Chapter 11: {1} Vines Complete Expository Dictionary of Bible Words © 1984 Thomas Nelson Pub. W.E. Vine
{2} Merriam Webster Collegiate Dictionary c 2006 Merriam Webster
{3} New Testament Greek Notebook (B. Chapman) p. 68
{4} American Heritage Dictionary, 5th edition c 2012 Dell mass market Ed.
{5} A Christian Manifesto – Francis Schaeffer C 1982 – Crossway - p. 50
{6} Christian Education – D. Sloat gen ed.@C1999 Moody Press
{7} Holloman Illustrated Bible Dictionary C2003 Holloman ref. A division of Holloman Bible Publishing

Chapter 12: {1}. The Faith – Charles W. Colson & Gary Poole, ©2008 Zondervan
{2} Christians in an Age of Outrage – Ed Stetzer, ©2008 Tyndale
{3} IBID
{4} The Biggest Lie in the History of Christianity – Matthew Kelly, ©2018 Kakadu LLC – Blue Sparrow Books

©2019 Dennis Orork

CPSIA information can be obtained
at www.ICGtesting.com
Printed in the USA
LVHW082301201121
703953LV00003B/42